D1161391

JOSEPH MOST JUST

OTHER BOOKS BY FATHER FILAS

Joseph Most Just

THEOLOGICAL QUESTIONS ABOUT ST. JOSEPH

FRANCIS L. FILAS, S.J., S.T.D.

THE BRUCE PUBLISHING COMPANY
MILWAUKEE

Imprimi potest:

    JOSEPHUS M. EGAN, S.J.
    Vice-Praepositus Provincialis

Nihil obstat:

    JOANNES A. SCHULIEN, S.T.D.
    Censor librorum

Imprimatur:

    ✠ ALBERTUS G. MEYER
    Archiepiscopus Milwauchiensis

    Die 4ᵃ Aprilis, 1956

Rosary College Dewey Classification Number: 232.932

Library of Congress Catalog Card Number: 56–9643

Like the two predecessors in this trilogy,
JOSEPH MOST JUST is gratefully dedicated
to the Immaculate Heart of the "Virgin
espoused to a man named JOSEPH" —
to Mary, Mother of the King of kings,
and
Mother of God.

Prefatory Note

JOSEPH MOST JUST was written to make available in English some of the developments in Catholic theology concerning St. Joseph's dignity, holiness, and privileges. This is intended to be more than a devotional book. It should provide a solid theological basis for devotion to St. Joseph, without becoming so technical as to be of use only to professional theologians.

Material already presented in *The Man Nearest to Christ* and *Joseph and Jesus* is not repeated here except where necessary by way of summary. However, to complement the historical data in *The Man Nearest to Christ,* the appendix offers a survey of the history of the devotion to St. Joseph since the middle 1500's, the period of the Council of Trent.

This book was made possible because of the literature at the Research and Documentation Center, St. Joseph's Oratory, Montreal, which was generously put at my disposal by the Reverend Emile Deguire, C.S.C., Superior of St. Joseph's Oratory. My deep gratitude is also extended to the Reverend Roland Gauthier, C.S.C., S.T.D., Director of the Center, who very kindly examined the manuscript and offered helpful suggestions and improvements.

FRANCIS L. FILAS, S.J.

Loyola University, Chicago, Illinois
Feast of the Sacred Heart, 1956

Abbreviations Used in References

AAS: *Acta Apostolicae Sedis.*

ASS: *Acta Sanctae Sedis.*

CJ: *Cahiers de Joséphologie,* Montreal.

DTC: Vacant-Mangenot-Amann, *Dictionnaire de théologie catholique.*

EJ: *Estudios Josefinos,* Valladolid.

JJ: Filas, *Joseph and Jesus.*

MNC: Filas, *The Man Nearest to Christ.*

QP: Leo XIII, *Quamquam Pluries, ASS* 22, 65.

SI: Vivès, *Summa Iosephina.*

ST: Thomas Aquinas, *Summa Theologiae.*

Contents

Contents

JOSEPH MOST JUST

CHAPTER ONE

Introductory Notions

VERY pertinently the questions might be asked, "What is the purpose of a study of the theology of St. Joseph? Should we not be content to accept St. Joseph merely as the protector of Mary and Jesus, calling him by the time-tested name of foster father? Or why seek more data, delving into Holy Scripture and Church history, since, as every thinking person can discover for himself, there is so little we know about the Saint? Why risk infringing on the rights of the eternal Father, perhaps detracting as well from the exclusive rank of the Blessed Virgin?"

The chief answer to these queries rests on the principle that knowledge is the basis for action. All other things being equal, we can love and imitate St. Joseph so much the more as we know more about him. Conversely, the greater our love, the greater will be our interest in learning all possible details of his dignity and of his holiness.

A second reason for scientific investigation is the pressing need to find exactly where the truth exists. Only too often in the past, authors' personal devotion to St. Joseph, praiseworthy in itself, has led them into untenable excesses in their writings. The Bollandist Hippolyte Delehaye, S.J., merely restates the historical record when he notes that "the clients of this great saint have so rarely succeeded in producing a work worthy of their subject."[1] A contemporary theologian, Boniface Llamera, O.P., remarks, "In many such works there predominate vagueness and imprecision, senti-

mentality and superfluity. They are works of great imagina-
tive labor, but of little fecundity and of little use for the
faithful."[2]

When we realize the consequences of uncritical works on
the Saint, we desire all the more a candid, realistic treatment.
Among Catholics the devotion to St. Joseph itself has suffered because of exaggerations and mental vagaries. Once a
person has been exposed to some of the rash and unfounded
claims made for the Saint, the danger is that thereafter he
will reject *a priori* whatever is said of St. Joseph, if it has
the slightest appearance of being new.

For non-Catholics, as we shall note later, uncritical writings on the Saint have been an occasion to extend criticism
to *all* Catholic doctrine in general. The biased critic has seen
in this field pious fancy and fruitless speculation. That errors
of such sort have existed, cannot and ought not be denied;
but serious research on St. Joseph should not be stigmatized
with censures that belong to ill-advised extremes.[3]

The correct attitude avoids criteria that err by excess or
defect. On the one hand we do not wish to build on pious
audacity, using principles rashly or wrongly proposed. On
the other hand excessive caution is equally out of place.
Even if we cannot reach absolute certitude in many cases,
theological deduction retains its scientific value in analyzing
the evidence that exists.

To a person unacquainted with modern writing on St.
Joseph, the use of terms such as "Josephite theology" or
"Josephology" may seem wholly novel or without precedent.
One reason for lack of acquaintance with these terms is the
fact that so little has appeared in English concerning the
Saint. But Latin, German, French, and Spanish writers have
systematized and co-ordinated the historical and doctrinal
matter referring to St. Joseph to such an extent that this
body of material has repeatedly received the name, "theology
of St. Joseph." Hocedez places its formal appearance in the
latter part of the nineteenth century, when together with

increased devotion to Mary, devotion to her virginal husband grew apace, and with it "what can be called the theology of St. Joseph, that is, the scientific study of his dignity, his mission, and his prerogatives."[4] Bibliographical evidence further indicates how prevalent is such usage. For example, Mueller calls his book "dogmatic foundations" of St. Joseph's cultus; Lepicier presents his contributions as a theological tractate; Macabiau arranges his material in the form of "theological theses"; and Bover subtitles his monograph, "a theological inquiry."[5] The French Dictionary of Catholic Theology uses the term on a level with other accepted wording: "The theology of St. Joseph is summed up in the study of the prerogatives of the Saint."[6]

By a parallel with the theology of Mary the title "Josephology" has already taken hold. Llamera, writing in 1944, admits that the title lacks wide use, but on the suggestion of "persons of authority" believes it should be accepted.[7] It would seem that this word "Josephology" will eventually find over-all usage, especially since the semiannual journal issued by the Research and Documentation Center at St. Joseph's Oratory, Montreal, has included it in its permanent title, Cahiers de Joséphologie.

As for the adjective "Josephite," it has long been accepted as good usage, in describing members of Congregations of Religious of St. Joseph. Hence, in evident preference to "Josephine" — which is the only other likely modifier — "Josephite" theology aptly refers to the theology of St. Joseph just as Marian theology refers to that of our Lady.

When we speak of the theology of St. Joseph, the question arises how such an expression can be justified inasmuch as theology would seem to be the science of God rather than the study of any of His creatures.[8] The reply is easy to give. Theology treats not only of God directly, but also of all other things in their relationships to their Creator, in so far as these relationships are known in the light of revelation. That is why we can properly define the theology of St.

Joseph as a branch of theological knowledge which, being founded on revealed principles, studies the Saint in his position as virginal husband of Mary and virgin father of Jesus, together with all the graces and privileges that flow from his double office.

It is, moreover, a branch of dogmatic theology because it is concerned with ordering knowledge to truth, and not truth to action, as does moral theology. It is also a subdivision of the theology of Mary; and Mariology in its turn is part of the treatise on Christ Incarnate. Schematically, the theology of St. Joseph considers the Saint:

first, in his relationship to Mary;

second, in his fatherly relationship to Jesus; and

third, as he possesses the graces, privileges, and holiness that grow out of this double vocation.

Like all parts of Catholic theology, Josephite theology should establish solid foundations for true devotion. The piety of the faithful should ultimately rest on its principles, using them as a guide either to check or to stimulate. The study also has great value because of Joseph's intimacy with Jesus and Mary. We investigate the Saint's position not only because his honor and glory redound to the honor and glory of Mary and thence to the honor and glory of Jesus, but also because Josephology helps us penetrate more deeply into the vast mystery of the Incarnation and into the awesome meaning of Mary's motherhood of God.

THE SOURCES

The general sources for the doctrinal study of St. Joseph are the same as in all theological inquiry. They are drawn from divine revelation, as explained and defended by human reason. In St. Joseph's case divine revelation has come to us through Holy Scripture, interpreted by Church teaching and Church writers.

So often the statement has been made that the Gospels tell us practically nothing about St. Joseph. True, they devote to him only a relatively few sentences, but the contents of these lines have tremendous implications. Our primary sources are the opening chapters of the Gospels of Matthew and Luke. The gospel doctrine can be listed under the following headings:

a) Joseph's genealogy[9];
b) his betrothal to Mary, and his justice[10];
c) the angel's revelation to him of Mary's miraculous conception[11];
d) the solemnization of his marriage to our Lady[12];
e) the trip to Bethlehem[13];
f) Joseph's presence at the adoration of the shepherds[14];
g) Joseph's naming of the Child Jesus[15];
h) Joseph's part at the presentation of Jesus[16];
i) the flight into Egypt and the return[17];
j) life at Nazareth[18];
k) the loss and finding of the Child in the Temple[19];
l) passing references to the Saint.[20]

This gospel doctrine can be summarized in four statements:

a) Joseph the carpenter is the husband of Mary, who is the virgin mother of Jesus.

b) Joseph was publicly thought to be the natural father of Jesus (until such time as Jesus proclaimed His divine origin).

c) Joseph exercised the office and held the rights of father of Jesus.

d) Joseph is explicitly singled out as a just man — a biblical expression that indicates he was adorned with virtue.

If we look to the official documents of the Church for further guidance, we find that nothing has been explicitly defined concerning the Saint. In other words no pronouncement exists which treats chiefly of him and at the same time has been solemnly declared by the Church to present a teaching revealed by God. However, a relatively long list can be made of papal decrees and letters which augmented the devotion to St. Joseph either in individual countries or throughout the entire Church.[21]

The outstanding pronouncement on St. Joseph is *Quamquam Pluries,* an encyclical of Leo XIII issued in 1889.[22] The most important document because of its consequences, however, is the decree of Pius IX which declared St. Joseph Patron of the Universal Church on December 8, 1870.[23] Leo XIII's letter on the Holy Family[24] and the 1920 letter of Benedict XV[25] are the only other papal documents addressed to the entire Church and dealing at length with St. Joseph. In 1937 Pius XI made the Saint patron of the Church's campaign against atheistic communism and thus brought to the fore another aspect of St. Joseph's patronage over the Universal Church.[26] On May 1, 1955, Pius XII instituted the feast of St. Joseph the Worker. The pontiff's announcement of the new feast warmly encouraged devotion to the Saint as to one most intimately linked with Christ.[27]

For the theologian, who distinguishes and classifies the dogmatic notes or values of various propositions, this source material cannot prove any truth respecting St. Joseph as matter defined of Catholic and divine faith — the highest value possible. However, these documents validly point out the mind of the Church.

To find further source material of Josephology, we turn to the writings of the Fathers of the Church. The testimony of the Fathers is valuable because these early churchmen serve as witnesses of Christian doctrine as handed down from Christ through the Apostles. When all the Fathers, or at least a majority of them, agree on some theological issue, adhering to it as a matter of divine faith, we are assured that their statements represent the teaching of Christ as interpreted during their era, covering the first six or seven Christian centuries. Of course, when the Fathers express their views only as private theologians, their opinions are to be given the same value accorded to the opinions of orthodox theologians today.

The reticence of the Fathers of the Church concerning St. Joseph is one of the most unusual and problematic features in the history of the devotion. As we have written elsewhere on this point, "If the devotion to the Saint had developed as other devotions in the Church have done, we would undoubtedly have been provided with copious material from the Fathers. But in actual fact, strong reasons existed which compelled an almost unbroken silence, relatively speaking, on the part of the Fathers. We must briefly consider these reasons here if we are to evaluate properly the scant attention which the Saint received in patristic times.

"It was the vocation of Joseph to protect the honor of Mary and of her Child, and to support them during the years which preceded the public life of our Lord. When the time came for Jesus to begin His teaching before the eyes of the world, Joseph had to fade into the background. If the Saint had been given special prominence, Jesus in His public life would have experienced additional difficulty in proving that His divine sonship was natural sonship. Therefore, according to the plans of God Joseph had to remain obscure.

"If this was the situation during the years of our Lord's apostolate, the same situation persisted perhaps to a greater extent during the first five hundred years of the Church. Implicitly, it seems, the Fathers felt that Joseph's singular relationship to Christ could not be emphasized without danger to the dogmas of the faith. However, two more cogent reasons for the Fathers' reticence also existed. The early Church was a church of martyrs, and except for the veneration of the Blessed Virgin, the martyrs were the ones who received religious honors from the faithful. Moreover, the pressure from contemporary heresies exerted a constant and powerful influence. These heresies attacked the bedrock doctrines of Christianity: the divinity of Christ and the true nature of the Trinity. To use a comparison, there could be no thought of guarding St. Joseph, the ornate frame of the portrait, as long as the safety was threatened of Jesus Christ and our Lady, the persons who constituted the priceless masterpiece itself."[28]

Because of these circumstances it can be understood that an explicit reference to the holiness or dignity of St. Joseph is all the more valuable when coming from the Fathers of the Church, since the Fathers did not intend to discuss the Saint *ex professo;* he was mentioned only in comments incidental to an explanation and defense of the gospel text. Such reticence actually provides an unimpeachable negative argument for St. Joseph. In common with the faithful of all ages and of all places in the Church, the Fathers never refused to grant the Saint his place as husband of Mary and "father" of Jesus according to the gospel account.

One possible exception to this statement is found in the case of those few Fathers who accepted parts of the apocryphal legends concerning the childhood of Mary and our Lady's relationship to St. Joseph. Their apparent denial of Joseph's position as Mary's husband is actually a denial of the use of marriage rights. The legends themselves invented many a story — for instance, Joseph's supposed advanced age — with the polemic intent of defending the dogma of Mary's virginity.

When modern writers discuss specific theological questions concerning St. Joseph (such as Joseph's assumption into heaven, his sinlessness, and other possible prerogatives), it is noticeable that they do not often invoke the Fathers of the Church as authorities concerning these *specific* topics. The reason is that the devotion came to maturity late in the life of the Church; and the theology of St. Joseph has similarly grown only in late centuries. The Fathers — particularly Jerome, Augustine, Ambrose, and Ephrem — have their importance when the foundations of the theology of St. Joseph are established, namely, the virginal marriage of Joseph and our Lady, and the true fatherhood which Joseph exercised in the moral order over Christ our Lord. The specific questions concerning Joseph's graces and privileges are advanced refinements of later times, deduced from the existence of these principles that act as the foundations of Josephite theology.

THE DIFFICULTY

At this point an objection arises which seems weighty indeed. We have been referring to the growth of the devotion to St. Joseph. Yet the Church is not allowed to change the doctrine it received from Christ, and admittedly, the devotion to St. Joseph did not exist publicly in the first twelve hundred years of the Church. How can the devotion be genuine, or in other words, how can the theology of St. Joseph be legitimate if the Saint was unknown for long centuries after the age of the Apostles?

The difficulty is by no means fanciful, nor is it to be minimized. It was very real for many Protestants who in 1889 bitterly criticized Leo XIII for having issued his great encyclical on St. Joseph.[29] Their argument against the devotion can be phrased in words like this: "Why was not St. Joseph always honored in the past? You claim that your church was founded by Christ, that it teaches only what Christ taught, and that it bases all its teachings on Holy Scripture and tradition. Isn't it true that Joseph was completely neglected in early Christian times? Why didn't the first Christians of the primitive Church perceive his greatness? They had the same Gospels, yet they did not pay St. Joseph respect in this modern way. Evidently, your Church has disobeyed Christ's commands. Somewhere along the line it has added to the Saviour's teachings, and has introduced the devotion to St. Joseph to cater to the pious sentiments of its members."

That this is an accurate summary of a Protestant position appears from the words of A. Lukyn Williams in a non-Catholic reference work. "However much," he writes, "we may respect the faith of Joseph and gladly recognize not only Paul the tent-maker and Peter the fisherman but also Joseph the carpenter as confessedly high examples of the dignity of work and of the spiritual reward it receives, we can have little sympathy with teaching that stands in such lurid contrast to the reticence of the Gospels and of the early Church."[30]

Williams should be given credit for having seen the historical contradictions that arose from certain exaggerated claims for St. Joseph which he met in a Catholic devotional writer. His comment is by no means in the same class with the pure fantasy of Salomon Reinach, who claimed that the cultus of St. Joseph was unknown during the Middle Ages, even during the Renaissance, and that it developed only in the nineteenth century because of Jesuit influences![31]

At any rate, all such objections fail to recognize the *basis* of the devotion to St. Joseph. The faithful as a body never refused to venerate St. Joseph. The Church at no time refused to preach the parts of the Gospel that referred to him, and in no instance did she ever make any declaration against the dignity and the holiness of his ministry. (We may use "ministry" as an accepted theological term to indicate Joseph's service of Jesus and Mary.) History is very clear on this point. For long centuries Joseph was never singled out. Today in our twentieth century he is still regarded in the same position he has always held as a servant of Christ and Mary in their private home life. Now, however, he is given special honor.

The objection, none the less, can recur in a new form. "Granted that the Church did not change its doctrine, it at least added something new in sanctioning the more advanced veneration of St. Joseph." And this is correct. There can be no objection to a new devotion as such, for in every devotion some special aspect of the Church's teaching is emphasized. Just where the emphasis is to be placed and to what degree, depends ultimately on the plans of Divine Providence.

In many cases we ourselves can discern the wisdom of God achieving His all-perfect ends. For example, all Catholics have always believed in the sacrament of the Holy Eucharist; but special devotion to the Blessed Sacrament did not appear until the thirteenth century. Again, in the seventeenth century when the freezing rigors of Jansenism threatened the Church, the devotion to the Sacred Heart was given us in order that the personal love of Jesus might be kept before men's eyes. In the case of our Blessed Lady, the devotion of the rosary was bestowed on the world when the world needed it. In every crisis of the Church Mary has been set forth as our chief intercessor with Christ according to some new devotion or according to a revival and continuation of an older one.

So it is in the case of St. Joseph. While admitting that we cannot fully understand God's reasons for postponing the devotion over so long a period, we are able to see the wisdom of the divine plan as it has been unfolded before us. St. Joseph was reserved for our times because our times need him as the saint of social justice and the saint of the family. Joseph the carpenter is to teach the value and dignity of labor, the holiness of marriage, respect for authority, social and interracial justice, and the critical importance of saintly family life — all vital issues that have to be stressed again and again in order to combat the modern errors of worship of the state, of wealth, of pleasure, and of power.

However, we must not deny the fact that the delay of the devotion to St. Joseph does create a problem. Why did the Church neglect Joseph so long in its public veneration? Various answers have been given, more or less along the lines already mentioned here. It will help to present several of these other approaches suggested by modern authors.

Cardinal Lepicier writes, "Many think that the cultus of St. Joseph should be given slight estimation, for they notice how long it was delayed in the Church — as if he whom we see practically neglected in antiquity would now be worthy of mediocre attention!" Lepicier then gives the usual reasons, that a cultus of St. Joseph in early centuries might well have endangered the dogmas of the divine origin of Jesus and the virginal motherhood of Mary. He proposes new ideas, however, in noting the parallel between the delayed cultus of our Lady (in primitive Christianity) and that of St. Joseph. This short delay in widespread public veneration of Mary has never been used to militate against devotion to her. Hence, even a much greater delay ought not to be used against St. Joseph.

"In this connection," he says, "proportionate application should be made of what we taught elsewhere on the delay in the cultus of the Virgin.[32] Just as it had to be postponed lest faith in Christ, the true God-Man, be put in peril, so was it wisely ordained that Joseph was not to be honored with an outstanding cultus lest the supernatural birth of Christ and consequently the singular glory of the Virgin Mother be overshadowed."[33]

Dusserre explains the problem by distinguishing between the terms "cultus" and "devotion."[34] Normally, he says, the two words are used interchangeably as synonyms. Strictly speaking, however, they have different connotations. A "devotion" refers to the respectful, tender, and trusting *attitude* which one manifests toward a saint by reason of his virtue and his greatness. "Cultus" on the other hand consists in the *recognition* and *use* of the intercessory power of the saint. Cultus is first private when individuals offer their private prayers to God through the saint. When cultus becomes public, it is manifested in official prayers and acts of the Church.

Devotion and cultus, therefore, are theoretically distinct. Practically considered, however, they are inseparable. A feeling of devotion first draws one's attention to a particular saint. Meditation on his greatness then serves to make explicit what had previously been merely implied. This is a sort of theological reflection that leads to a growth in devotion, which in turns leads to cultus.

In other words one must first know a saint in order to admire and love him, and that is devotion. The next step is to invoke his intercession, and that is cultus. When cultus on the part of individuals has acquired mature status, it can then (with the approbation of the Church) become official and public cultus. But the two will ever go hand in hand so that cultus will be nourished by devotion, and devotion is vivified by cultus.

Dusserre continues: To apply these notions to St. Joseph: Private *devotion* to the Saint, in the sense just explained, was quite certainly in existence in the early Church although to a limited degree. Perhaps even a private cultus flourished. The writings of Jerome, Augustine, Ephrem, and Chrysostom prove that individuals were not lacking who discerned the outstanding virtue of St. Joseph. In the later Middle Ages, i.e., from the thirteenth century onward, private devotion to the Saint and private cultus to the Saint spread extensively.[35] Thus, for Dusserre the devotion to St. Joseph as well as the Saint's cultus is a development from private to public status. Logically, in this sense the devotion would always have been present in the Church.

Cardinal Newman is among those who have commented at length on the problem of the long delay of the devotion. He solves the difficulty by distinguishing between "faith" (or doctrine) and "devotion." Faith represents the Creed, the rule of faith, and the acceptance of that rule. Devotion represents the religious cultus which is attached to the objects of our faith, and the practice of that cultus. Devotion must presuppose faith, but faith does not necessarily lead to devotion. We can believe without feeling sentiments of devotion. Faith is one, always the same everywhere. Devotions have multiplied, are varied and variable. They wax and wane with the centuries.

Newman's analysis is quite lengthy, but merits practically full quotation because of its value and its pertinence. "The diversified modes of honoring God," he writes, "did not come to us in a day or only from the apostles; they are the accumulations of centuries; and, as in the course of years some of them spring up, so others decline and die. . . . The first of these sacred observances were the devotions paid to the apostles, then those which were paid to the martyrs; yet there were saints nearer to our Lord than either martyrs or apostles; but, as if these sacred persons were immersed and lost in the effulgence of His glory, and because they did not manifest themselves when in the body in external works separate from Him, it happened that for a long while they were less dwelt upon. . . .

"Hence at length those luminous stars rose in the ecclesiastical heavens, which were of more august dignity than any which had preceded them, and were late in rising, for the very reason that they were so specially glorious. Those names, I say, which at first sight might have been expected to enter soon into the devotions of the faithful, with better reason might have been looked for at a later date, and actually were late in their coming. St. Joseph furnishes the most striking instance of this remark; here is the clearest of instances of the distinction between doctrine and devotion. Who, from his prerogatives and the testimony on which they come to us, had a greater claim to receive an early recognition among the faithful than he? A saint of scripture, the foster father of our Lord, he was an object of the universal and absolute faith of the Christian world from the first, yet the devotion to him is of comparatively late date. When once it began, men seemed surprised that it had not been thought of before; and now they hold him next to the Blessed Virgin in their religious affection and veneration."[36]

A final quotation, from Frederick William Faber, merits inclusion here. He writes, "The adoration of Jesus and the devotion to Mary had taken their places immovably in the

sense of the faithful and in the practical system of the
Church, one shedding light upon the other, and both instructing, illuminating, nourishing, and sanctifying the people. But there was still one more of the 'Earthly Trinity' as
it is called.

"Devotion to St. Joseph lay, as it were, dormant in the
Church. Not that there was anything new to be known about
him, or any fresh revelation to be made of him, except in the
way of private revelations to the saints. He belonged exclusively to the sacred infancy. The beginnings of St. Matthew's
Gospel contained him. By two evangelists he had been left in
complete silence, and the third had barely named him in the
genealogy. Tradition held some scanty notices of him; but
they had no light but what they had borrowed from St.
Matthew. All we have now of St. Joseph was there then; only
the sense of the faithful had not taken it up; God's time was
not yet come. The sense of the faithful was not like the complete science of the apostles. It was not equal to it; it had to
grow it; to master it, to fill it out with devotion, to animate
it with institutions, to submit it as a perfectly administered
hierarchy. But God's time came for this dear devotion; and
it came like all His gifts when times were dark and calamities
were rife."[37]

These explanations of the delay in the devotion to St.
Joseph can be summed up in terms of Newman's distinction
between doctrine and devotion. Doctrines relating to the
vocation and dignity of St. Joseph are unmistakably founded
on Holy Scripture. The devotion rests on these doctrines. It
has changed throughout the years in the sense that after its
appearances it has become more explicit and detailed. In
itself it does not belong to the substantials of the Faith, but
the doctrines on which it is founded have remained ever the
same.

THE PLAN OF THIS BOOK

Not all the subjects included in the theology of St. Joseph
are to be discussed in the following pages. We omit here the

rather theoretical questions whether and where St. Joseph is prefigured in the Old Testament, and precisely what gifts of grace he possessed in detail. Nor is this the place to study at great length the nature of St. Joseph's marriage to our Lady as well as his fatherly relationship to Jesus. These subjects have already been covered elsewhere, and from this fuller treatment we can abstract the following ideas to summarize Joseph's position as husband and father.[38]

Joseph and Mary were linked in a true marriage although they made theirs a virginal marriage. Evidently by divine inspiration they voluntarily promised God not to make use of their matrimonial rights. It is the traditional and practically unanimous opinion among both Catholic and non-Catholic scholars that this valid marriage began at the moment of the espousal of Joseph and Mary, according to contemporary Jewish custom. There is some disagreement on how complete a marriage was effected by the espousal; but the fact that the marriage was at least essentially valid at the espousal seems to be so probable as to be practically certain.[39]

Following St. Thomas, we hold that "the marriage was specially ordained for this purpose, that the Child should be received and brought up within it."[40] God brought the marriage into existence for the express purpose of receiving and rearing Jesus in its midst. "In other words, the Child Jesus was truly the fruit, albeit miraculous, of the virginal marriage of Joseph and Mary. The holy couple exercised a joint parenthood even though Joseph's fatherhood, unlike the motherhood of Mary, was merely a moral and not a physical relationship."[41] Thus it is that the relationship of Joseph to Jesus comes to the Saint through and because of the marriage.

This fatherhood of the Saint by no means implies that Joseph had generated Jesus. It represents an analogical use of the word. It refers to the spiritual bond which ideally should unite every natural father and son, a bond which normally is based on the generation of the son by the father.

In the case of St. Joseph, since generation was absent, his bond to Jesus is something miraculous. None the less, his fatherly relationship stands for true parenthood, because the education and rearing of a child is looked on as a continuation or prolongation of the generative act; and God gave Joseph the task of educating and rearing the Child Jesus as if Jesus had been Joseph's natural son.

Since Jesus was given to the marriage of Joseph and our Lady, He becomes the miraculous fruit of the marriage, and on this score St. Joseph is called Jesus' father in the moral order, by right of marriage. Such a fatherhood is concerned not with the physical act of generation but with the reception of Jesus and with His rearing. It includes the paternal love and service which traditionally have been described by the title of foster father. To correspond with such love, God gave St. Joseph his authority as head of the Holy Family. Because of it Joseph has been called "virgin father of Jesus" — a title indicating he is father of Christ in so far as he, a virginal man, can be the father of Jesus. This echoes the interpretation of many Christian centuries that Joseph was father of Jesus in all respects with the sole exception of physical generation.

Such, then, are the key ideas of Joseph's marriage and fatherhood. They are critically important as a sort of first premise for all Josephology. All later discussions and all future claims for Joseph's holiness and privileges grow out of them. Leo XIII himself makes it clear how fundamental is this position of Joseph as husband and father. In the encyclical *Quamquam Pluries* the pope states, "Blessed Joseph . . . was indeed the husband of Mary and the father, as was supposed, of Jesus Christ. *From this arise all his dignity, grace, holiness, and glory.* . . . [The Church] is his numberless family, scattered throughout all lands, over which he rules with a sort of paternal authority, because he is the husband of Mary and the father of Jesus Christ."[42]

OUR METHOD

In the following pages we shall present many deductions from the fact of Joseph's double office. Because of the relatively scanty source material concerning the Saint, our answers to certain theological questions must come either by means of such direct deductions or indirectly by means of an argument from analogy. Properly used, such logic can lead and does lead to reliable information. For example, with respect to the argument from analogy, we know of the existence of certain privileges of the saints. What belongs to the saints in general, must by a stronger reason — granting Joseph's exalted position — belong to St. Joseph. Yet this does not mean that all the *particular* privileges of all the saints will be attributed to the virgin father of Jesus. God bestows special graces suited to the needs of special apostolates, and Joseph was given all the helps he required. He might have lacked the special gift of miraculous preaching which the Apostles needed and received for their first exacting tasks; but he must have been given in outstanding measure every *generic* gift which every saint would receive.

By a converse use of this analogy we can also ask whether or not the sublime privileges of Mary belong to Joseph in a lesser degree. Many of the graces of Mary were granted her specifically to help her in her parental task. Reasonably, then, God must have bestowed similar graces on Joseph because Joseph's task was also that of a parent. Joseph's fatherhood in the moral order is unique; hence, his graces like Mary's must also be unique. Nevertheless, in reasoning in this way we must be most diligent lest any grace given exclusively to Mary would seem, by improper logic, to be shared with even so holy a man as Mary's husband.

Such in brief outline is the argument from analogy. It merges into the argument from direct deduction, setting down Joseph's vocation as its major premise:

"According to Holy Scripture and official documents of

the Church, St. Joseph was chosen to be the virginal husband of our Lady, the virgin father of Jesus, the head of the Holy Family, and the patron of the Universal Church."

Then follows the minor premise:

"However, implicitly included in this vocation *because required by it* are various privileges and graces."

To conclude:

"Hence, these privileges belong to St. Joseph."

Our first consideration will be the dignity of St. Joseph's position. Next, the fact of his dignity implicitly indicates the holiness which his position demanded. With regard to the Saint's holiness we will ask the detailed questions when and how his sanctity was acquired; how it was conserved and increased; and finally, how it was rewarded. The concluding chapters will describe his position in the Church today: his patronage over all, and the reasons suggesting that the Church will eventually grant him greater honors in its liturgy.

REFERENCES — CHAPTER ONE

1. Hippolyte Delehaye, S.J., In *Analecta Bollandiana*, 28 (1909), 313.

2. Bonifacio Llamera, O.P., "Introducción a la teología de San José," in *Ciencia Tomista*, 66 (1944), 259.

3. Among other writers echoing these ideas are Cyprian Macabiau ("C.M." and "C. Mariani"), *De Cultu Sancti Josephi Amplificando* (Paris: Lethielleux, 1908), xi; Eugenio Cantera, O.A.R., *San José en el plan divino*, Santa Rita, Monachii, 1917, vi, 18; Joseph Seitz, *Die Verehrung des heiligen Joseph* (Freiburg im Breisgau: Herder, 1908), vi.

4. Edgar Hocedez, S.J., *Histoire de la Théologie au XIXᵉ Siècle* (Paris: Desclée de Brouwer, 1947), 3, 317.

5. Joseph Mueller, S.J., *Der heilige Joseph — Die dogmatischen Grundlagen seiner besonderen Verehrung* (Innsbruck: Rauch, 1937); A. H. Card. Lepicier, O.S.M., *Saint Joseph, Epoux de la très sainte Vierge* (Paris: Lethielleux, 1932), and also *Tractatus de Sancto Joseph* (Paris: Lethielleux, 1908) (3 ed., Rome, 1933); Macabiau, *op. cit.*; Joseph M. Bover, S.J., *De Cultu Sancti Josephi Amplificando* (Barcelona: Subirana, 1926); Henri Rondet, S.J., *Saint Joseph, Textes Anciens avec une Introduction* (Paris: Lethielleux, 1954); Bonifacio Llamera, O.P., *Teología de San José*, La editorial catolica, Madrid, 1954.

6. A. Michel, "Joseph, Saint," in *DTC*, 8, 1510.

7. Llamera (*Ciencia Tomista*), 265.

8. The material in this section is built on Cantera, 1–10; Llamera, 255–275; and *idem*, "La paternidad de San José en la teología católica," in *EJ*, 5 (1951), 205–211.

9. Mt. 1:1–16; Lk. 3:23–38.

10. Mt. 1:18–19; Lk. 1:27.

11. Mt. 1:20–23.

12. Mt. 1:24–25.

13. Lk. 2:1–7.

14. Lk. 2:16.

15. Mt. 1:25; Lk. 2:21.

16. Lk. 2:22–36.

17. Mt. 2:13–23.

18. Mt. 2:23; Lk. 2:39, 51.

19. Lk. 2:41–50.

20. Mt. 13:55; Lk. 4:22; Jn. 1:45; 6:42.

21. A list of most of these decrees is contained in *MNC*, 195–199.

22. Leo XIII, *Quamquam Pluries*, *AAS*, 22, 65.

23. Pius IX, *Quemadmodum Deus*, *ASS*, 6, 193.

24. Leo XIII, *Neminem Fugit*, Decr. No. 3777, C.S.R.

25. Benedict XV, *Bonum Sane*, *AAS*, 12, 313.

26. Pius XI, *Divini Redemptoris*, *AAS*, 29, 106. English translations of these five documents can be found in *MNC*, 162–185.

27. Pius XII, address (in Italian) on the occasion of the tenth anniversary of the Christian Association of Italian Workers, May 1, 1955; quoted in *L'Osservatore Romano*, May 2–3, 1955; *AAS*, 47 (1955), 402–407; English translation in *Catholic Documents* (London: Salesian Press), No. 18, July, 1955, 31–35; also in Rondet-Attwater, *Saint Joseph* (New York: Kenedy, 1956), 222–226.

28. *JJ*, 4–5. For a fuller explanation of the legends of St. Joseph and their polemical purpose, as well as a refutation of their claim, cf. *MNC*, 7–41.

29. Macabiau, 39.

30. A. Lukyn Williams, "Joseph, Saint," in *Hastings' Dictionary of the Bible* (New York: Scribner, 1902), 2, 777.

31. Salomon Reinach, *Orpheus* (London: Routledge, 1931), 418.

32. Alexis Lepicier, O.S.M., *Tractatus de B.M.V. Matre Dei*, P. 3, c. 2, art. 2, n. 15, 2; the same doctrine is found in Dom Gaston Démaret, O.S.B., *Marie de qui est né Jésus*, tom. 6, "Saint Joseph" (Paris: Spes, 1939), 313, who follows Lépicier quite closely.

33. Alexis Lépicier, O.S.M., *Tractatus de S. Joseph*, Rome, 1933, 330–331.

34. Joseph Dusserre, "Les origines de la dévotion à saint Joseph," in *CJ*, 1 (1953), 24.

35. With the introduction of the feast of St. Joseph in the Roman church in 1479, the cultus first became official and public, at least for the area within which the feast was permitted. Cf. *MNC*, 151; Seitz, 211.

36. J. H. Cardinal Newman, *Certain Difficulties Felt by Anglicans* (New York: Longmans, 1891), 2, 26; 2, 30–31.

37. Frederick William Faber, *The Blessed Sacrament* (London: Burns, Oates), no date, 170–174.

38. This summary is based on *JJ*, 10–19 and 128–165.

39. Cf. Bernard G. Murchland, C.S.C., in *CJ*, 1 (1953), 134, for a summary of the most advanced view as to the degree of completeness of the marriage. The present author proposed the minority opinion, i.e., that the espousal was equivalent to a sort of engagement, in *MNC*, 62. This was retracted in *JJ*, 20.

40. Aquinas, *In IV Sent.*, d. 30, q. 2, a. 2 ad 4.

41. *JJ*, 129.   42. *MNC*, 171.

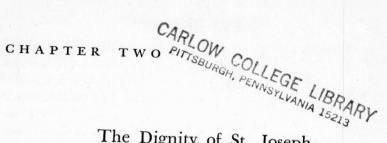

The Dignity of St. Joseph

DIGNITY always implies some sort of excellence, and this excellence in its turn arises from the possession of a good or of a perfection. Hence it is that "a person becomes more excellent by the fact that he possesses a good more excellently than others do."[1] Here we have a general truth which we can use in two ways in understanding the dignity of St. Joseph, either considering the excellence of the Saint in itself, or considering it in respect to the excellence of other persons.

We go to Thomas Aquinas for the principles from which to deduce St. Joseph's true dignity. Aquinas himself did not apply these principles to St. Joseph; he used them to construct his theology concerning the dignity and holiness of Mary. He wrote, "Those whom God chooses for an office, He prepares and disposes in such a way that they become suited to it, according to the saying of St. Paul, 'He has made us fit ministers of the New Covenant' (2 Cor. 3:6). But the Blessed Virgin was divinely chosen to be the Mother of God, and therefore there can be no doubt that God fitted her for this position by means of His grace."[2]

Joseph, like Mary, was chosen for an office — the headship of the Holy Family. He must, then, have been divinely prepared and disposed in order to be suited for it. Therefore, "there can be no doubt that God fitted" Joseph for his responsibility. Joseph's excellence arose because God selected him; it was increased or, so to speak, confirmed because

God's grace helped him live out his exalted position worthily. Any difficulties would arise not so much in the application of this principle to Joseph himself, but rather in questioning the truth of the principle. For example, was Judas the traitor divinely chosen like Joseph and Mary? With Terrien, we must answer that Judas was indeed chosen by God, but not as were St. Joseph and our Lady. "If there was a liar among the apostles chosen by Jesus Christ in person, this is because the choice of Judas was not absolute. The Lord, in calling Judas to follow Him, knew He would be betrayed by him, but even this went along with the plans of His mercy since the salvation of the world demanded that He be delivered."[3] In the case of St. Joseph we realize that he did not become a traitor. The Gospels make it clear he fulfilled his God-given task perfectly, and all subsequent Catholic interpretation of the Gospels vouches for the Saint's fidelity. That is how we know he worthily fulfilled the vocation to which God called him and for which God prepared him.

St. Thomas applied a second principle to our Lady which we again refer in a parallel way to St. Joseph. "To the degree that something approaches its source," Aquinas wrote, "by so much does it participate in the effect of that source. . . . Christ is the source of grace. . . . The Blessed Virgin Mary was the closest to Christ in His humanity, because He took His human nature of her. Hence, in preference to all other people she had to receive the fulness of grace from Christ."[4] But Joseph was closest to Mary and to Jesus because of his position as husband and father. Therefore, reasoning from the general rule, we would suppose that Joseph had to receive the "fulness of grace" second of course to Mary; and again second to Mary, his dignity would be "in preference to all other people."

Strictly speaking, this closeness to Jesus as the source of grace would argue great *holiness* for St. Joseph. It would not *directly* indicate his *dignity*, if by "dignity" we mean the excellence Joseph possessed because of his vocation. Admittedly, Joseph's holiness of itself is already an excellence or dignity. But here we are looking first at St. Joseph's vocation, at the honored rank it brought to the Saint, at his "dignity," and not yet at his "holiness" or likeness to God.

One can reasonably wonder why there seems to be this lack of clear-cut determination in the question of St. Joseph's dignity contrasted with his holiness. Perhaps the cause for the confusion is that one is not precisely the other, but they do go hand in hand. The dignity of St. Joseph required that he be proportionately holy if he was to be worthy of his vocation. His holiness in its turn, as second to the holiness of Mary, would give Joseph an excellence far surpassing the dignity of any other created being except again our Lady.

ST. JOSEPH'S DIGNITY AS HUSBAND OF MARY

To arrive at a true idea of the dignity of Mary's husband, we take for granted a general appreciation of the true dignity of Mary, for that is the norm. God certainly did not choose an unworthy man to be the husband of the virgin Mother of God, linked so closely to the mystery of God becoming man. In the words ascribed to St. John Damascene, Joseph's position with respect to our Lady is "conceded to St. Joseph by the singular gift of God and by a dispensation that surpasses all understanding."[5]

Probably the best summary of this is found in Leo XIII's encyclical, *Quamquam Pluries*. "The dignity of the Mother of God," Leo says, "is certainly so sublime that nothing can surpass it. None the less, since the bond of marriage existed between Joseph and the Blessed Virgin, there can be no doubt that more than any other person he approached that supereminent dignity by which the Mother of God is raised far above all created natures."

The reason for such sharing always rests in the marriage between these two. "For marriage is the closest possible union and relationship whereby each spouse mutually participates in the goods of the other. Consequently, if God gave Joseph as a spouse to the Virgin, He assuredly gave him not only as a companion in life, a witness of her virginity, and the guardian of her honor, but also *as a sharer in her exalted dignity by reason of the conjugal tie itself.*"[6]

Reflection on the consequences of the marriage bond reveals constantly deeper meaning. For instance, when Mary visited Elizabeth, her cousin exclaimed, "How have I deserved that the mother of my Lord should come to me?" (Lk. 1:43.) Yet the visit of Mary to Elizabeth was something brief and temporary. If, even as such, it was to be considered such a magnificent honor, what must be the honor of living with Mary in the intimacy of family life for some thirty years, a privilege that only Joseph possessed as Mary's husband and for which he alone was chosen?

Moreover, because of the marriage our Lady was subject to St. Joseph. St. Paul says of matrimony that the "husband is head of the wife as Christ is head of the Church" (Eph. 5:23). Joseph, then, was in authority over Mary. His dignity on this score can be surpassed only by the fact that Jesus, too, was subject to the Saint. By reason of Mary's holiness and her vocation as Mother of God, our Lady was God's choicest creature, the living Ark of the Covenant. Providence entrusted this treasure to St. Joseph to be protected and cherished. No other creature, either angel or human, ever had so responsible a relationship.

Joseph's excellence also stands out by a consideration of the ties of love that existed between the Saint and our Lady. The fact is that Mary loved Joseph as she has never loved any other creature. She would not have been perfect in her vocation as the virgin wife of St. Joseph if her love for her husband had been surpassed by any other human affection. Conversely, Joseph as husband was bound to love Mary as he loved no other except God Himself. Joseph became the only created person to hold the primacy of Mary's love and to return it.

Comparisons and considerations such as these serve as apt norms to judge Joseph's dignity as husband. Still another comparison can bring home the idea even more strongly. Spiritual writers have long marveled at the dignity of St. John the Evangelist because Jesus put Mary into John's keeping on Calvary. The same warmth of expression should be extended to St. Joseph with greater force. John received Mary from her dying Son to guard her, to love her as his mother, to console her for her relatively few remaining years. Joseph had received Mary and guarded her and loved her as his virgin wife for the long years before she became a widow. One wonders why the force of this comparison between the privilege of Joseph and the privilege of John the Evangelist has been so little developed. Its *a fortiori* logic is powerful, striking, and clear.

Thus it is that we return to the fact that God chose St. Joseph to be the husband of our Lady, and God considered the Saint worthy of such a post. The Church put this idea into the oration for the former feast of the Solemnity of St. Joseph: "O God, who in thine ineffable providence was pleased to choose blessed Joseph as the spouse of thy most holy mother. . . ." In other words God foresaw Joseph's cooperation and bestowed on him the position in the Holy Family. As we earlier mentioned from St. Thomas, the marriage of the Saint and our Lady was expressly brought into existence by God in order to serve the Incarnation. The only man God chose for the husband was St. Joseph, to parallel the divine selection of Mary.

ST. JOSEPH'S DIGNITY AS FATHER OF JESUS

In analyzing the relationship of Joseph to Jesus, we are struck by the many parallels with Joseph's relationship to Mary. So, too, the consideration of the dignity of one parallels the dignity of the other. This is the plan Leo XIII follows. After discussing the marriage, the pope says, "Likewise,

Joseph *alone* stands out in august dignity because he was the guardian of the Son of God by the divine appointment, and in the opinion of men was His father. As a consequence, the Word of God was modestly obedient to Joseph, was attentive to his commands, and paid him every honor that children should render their parent."[7]

The pope's words provide headings under which Joseph's dignity as foster father can be listed. He was the "guardian of the Son of God by the divine appointment." This was no casual choice, no position obtained by accident. "In the opinion of men he was His father." Joseph had the tremendous honor of being selected as legal father, bound to Jesus by the legal and spiritual ties of fatherhood. And "as a consequence" Joseph received from Jesus the love and reverence and "every honor" owed to a true parent — which in a true sense Joseph must have been! Yet this child was no ordinary person; He was God Himself, the Son of God, and the son of Joseph. Joseph possessed His love as no other created person save Mary possessed it. Jesus was the perfect son; that is why we can know for certain that He loved Joseph in a manner and to a degree that He loved no one else, again excepting Mary. The reason is always the same: only one creature named Joseph of Nazareth, a carpenter, held the rights of father over Jesus Christ.

Joseph, then, was the father of Jesus not only in name and in popular estimation but also in actual fact. Theologians have not been slow to draw the parallel between Mary's motherhood and Joseph's fatherhood in the moral order. If the former gave Mary a quasi-infinite dignity because it had to do with God Himself, then with proper qualifications the other gave Joseph a quasi-infinite dignity because his fatherly relationship, too, referred to God.[8]

The dignity of the Saint continues to appear from the fact that Jesus was subject to him. This means that Joseph taught Jesus much of the experimental knowledge Jesus deigned to learn in His human nature. It also means that in a correct sense Joseph was the only man who ever possessed fatherly authority over God! The subjection must be understood, of course, with proper theological distinctions. Jesus was subject only with regard to His human nature and human will, not as to His divine nature and divine will. Again, He was subject not in strict rigor but rather by a condescension whereby He freely willed to be subject to Joseph. Finally, His obedience did not cover His divine mission as Saviour, as He indicated at the time He was found in the temple (Lk. 2:49). His was the submission of the child to its father, to show to the world the example of obedience in children who have not yet been emancipated from such obedience by mature age, marriage, or religious vows.[9]

Whether we look on Joseph's fatherhood from the aspect of Joseph's authority, his love for Jesus, or the selflessness it entailed, all considerations must end in superlatives. To use a comparison, Jesus praised John the Baptist (Mt. 11:11) superlatively because of the Baptist's utter abnegation in following out his vocation as herald of the Messias. But if Joseph's vocation had called for notice during the Public Life, what would have been the praise Jesus would give Joseph! The perfect "human father" of the perfect Son would wear himself out in the service of his charge. Jesus promised a reward for even a cup of water given to one of His "little ones" (Mt. 10:42), for this was evidently a noble action. St. Joseph gave not just one cup of water but his life and his service directly to Jesus.

Mueller suggests the comparison that St. Joseph's dignity as virgin father of Jesus gives the Saint greater excellence than sanctifying grace and the right to the beatific vision itself.[10] This refers, of course, only to the two *dignities* — the fatherly relationship to Jesus compared with the adoptive sonship of God in the supernatural order. It does not mean that Joseph's fatherhood *in itself* would give the Saint greater supernatural perfection, nor that *in itself* the fatherhood would make Joseph capable of that happiness which comes because of sanctifying grace and the beatific vision. Instead, the comparison points out that Joseph possesses true fatherly rights over Jesus; that Joseph is not the adoptive father, for Jesus is given to him within the bonds of his own marriage;[11] and therefore, the dignity of this true fatherhood of Him who is God is much greater than the dignity of being an adopted son of God.

Moreover, the beatific vision is something that belongs to God alone by nature. Adoptive sonship gives men and angels the right to share in the beatific vision. But Joseph's fatherhood would certainly give the Saint a stronger right to the beatific vision than would adoptive sonship.[12] The fatherhood is in a true sense the source of Joseph's graces.

A fitting conclusion to such reflections on the dignity of Joseph's fatherhood can best be made in the words of St. Bernard, adopted by the Church as a prayer in preparation for Mass: "O fortunate man, blessed Joseph, to whom it was given to see the God whom many kings yearned to see and did not see; to hear the God whom many kings yearned to hear and did not hear; not only to see and hear, but to carry, to kiss, to clothe and protect Him!"[13]

JOSEPH'S DIGNITY AS HEAD OF THE HOLY FAMILY

Perhaps, strictly speaking, St. Joseph's position as head of the Holy Family should not be considered a separate title to dignity so much as a combination of the other two, but it has its own special value. It depicts Joseph's relationship to Mary and Jesus *together*, not separately as "husband" and "father" do. Leo XIII evidently considers it a separate title, giving it prominence by itself: "From this double dignity [of husband and father] such duties arose as are prescribed by nature for the head of a household, so that Joseph was at once the legitimate and natural guardian, preserver, and defender of the divine household over which he presided. These duties he fulfilled as long as he lived. Zealously he watched over his spouse and her divine Child with the most ardent love and constant solicitude. By his labor he regularly provided for both of them such necessities of life as food and clothing. In seeking a place of refuge he warded off that danger to their lives which had been engendered by the jealousy of a king. Amid the inconveniences of the journey and the bitterness of exile he continually showed himself the companion, the helper, the consoler of the Virgin and of Jesus."[14]

This passage of the encyclical emphasizes the *natural* position of Joseph in the Holy Family. Again we are reminded that it is not something artificial and arbitrary, as if he were merely a protector of Mary and an adoptive guardian of Jesus. Instead, by the natural law itself Joseph governs the family whose other members are God and the Mother of God. The dignity he would have because of this authority has already been noted separately concerning the subjection of Mary and Jesus to Joseph; it is part of the ministry of the personal service of God Himself.

Suarez analyzed Joseph's place in the Holy Family by saying that the Saint thus participated in the "order of the hypostatic union." The word "hypostatic" comes from the Greek language, and means "personal." Hence, because the divine and human nature were united in the one *person* of Jesus Christ, the order of the hypostatic union refers essentially to the human nature of Jesus together with all the gifts, privileges, and relationships that directly flow from it.[15] Joseph and Mary also belong to the order of the hypostatic union, although not essentially but by reason of their ministries. Joseph's place lifts him above all other creatures because no one served Jesus and Mary more intimately than he. In the words of Suarez, "There are ministries which touch the order of the hypostatic union, and this order of its very nature is of higher perfection. . . . It is in this order that I think St. Joseph's ministry was instituted, and, as it were, in the lowest grade. But by the same token Joseph's position surpasses all others because it exists in this higher order."[16]

JOSEPH'S DIGNITY AS PATRON OF THE UNIVERSAL CHURCH

Earlier writers on St. Joseph could not discuss Joseph's universal patronage as a title of his dignity inasmuch as the official proclamation was not made until 1870. However, it is surprising that more recent theologians have not given it the separate attention it deserves. As in the case of "Head of the Holy Family," Joseph's patronage of the Church grows out of his fundamental position of husband and therefore father. Again according to Leo XIII, "The divine household which Joseph governed just as with paternal authority contained the beginnings of the new Church. The Virgin most holy is the mother of all Christians since she is the mother of Jesus and since she gave birth to them on the mount of Calvary amid the unspeakable sufferings of the Redeemer. Jesus is, as it were, the firstborn of Christians, who are His brothers by adoption and redemption. From these considerations we conclude that the blessed Patriarch must regard all the multitude of Christians who constitute the Church as confided to his care in a certain special manner. This is his numberless family, scattered throughout all lands, over which he rules with a sort of paternal authority because he is the husband of Mary and the father of Jesus Christ. Thus, it is conformable to reason and in every way becoming to Blessed Joseph that as once it was his sacred trust to guard with watchful care the family of Nazareth, no matter what befell, so now by virtue of his heavenly patronage he is in turn to protect and to defend the Church of Christ."[17]

Joseph's patronage of the Church is something unique, shared with him by no other saint. Michael the Archangel and the Apostles Peter and Paul do not have ranks so exalted. Michael's task is that of a quasi-military protector (cf. p. 90); Peter and Paul are the foundations of the Church at

Rome; but only Joseph is, if one can use the expression,
"father of the Church." As Leo XIII pointed out, it is this
note of fatherly protection that characterizes Joseph's patronage — fatherly love for everyone, everywhere in that Church
which is the outgrowth of the family at Nazareth. It is all the
more excellent because it is so universal, and because it is
based on Joseph's original vocation and his attitude toward
the Church.

This position of St. Joseph, indicated by the Church
documents in so many ways as second only to that of Mary,
appears also in the Office of the feast of St. Joseph the
Worker. There, the hymn for Lauds reads as follows:

> Altis locatus sedibus
> *Celsaeque Sponsae proximus,*
> Adesto nunc clientibus
> Quos vexat indigentia.
>
> Thou, high in heaven,
> *Closest to thy exalted spouse,*
> Help, now, thy clients
> Whom want presses sorely.

ST. JOSEPH AND THE ANGELS

All these reflections on Joseph's dignity as husband of
Mary, virgin father of Jesus, head of the Holy Family, and
patron of the Universal Church lead to the conclusion that
Joseph's worth is far greater than that of any other saint,
and evidently greater than the angels as well. But this suggested greatness requires an explicit comparison with the
angels and the greatest of the saints. Several difficulties arise
and would remain unanswered unless such a comparative
analysis is made.

An inquiry such as this does not flow, therefore, from idle
curiosity that tries to count the gifts of God as bestowed on
His servants. The wrong attitude would be that criticized in

the *Imitation of Christ:* "Do not be inquisitive or dispute concerning the merits of the saints; who is more holy than another, or who greater in the kingdom of heaven. Such often breed strifes and unprofitable contention and nourish also pride and vainglory whence arise envies and dissensions while one man proudly prefers this saint and another that" (3, 58).

It is true that rash statements on the relative dignity or holiness of the saints ought to be avoided, especially when data of revelation are absent. In the case of St. Joseph, however, the fonts of revelation contain enough information to draw conclusions that are reasonably certain. Such conclusions are not necessarily taught as of divine faith, but they can claim theological certainty or at least probability according to the reasoning behind them. Perhaps we should emphasize once again that the purpose of discussing the questions on the comparative dignity of St. Joseph is *not* to diminish the glory of the angels and other saints. The comparison is made necessary on another score. The evidence indicates that St. Joseph possesses exceptional dignity second to Mary. How are we to square this fact with the dignity or holiness of other saints?

The proper starting point for all discussion is undoubtedly the statement in the encyclical of Leo XIII, "There can be no doubt that more than any other person [St. Joseph] approached that supereminent dignity by which the Mother of God is raised far above all created natures."[18] Michel comments on the passage as follows: "To take these words in their full sense it would be necessary to conclude to the preeminence of St. Joseph not only above all the saints but above the angels." He adds, however, that the assertion should be interpreted as indicating the mind of the Church, and in a situation like this where so sweeping a claim is made, the greatest prudence should be manifested.[19] Interestingly enough Michel himself published a much less reserved interpretation some years before his opinion was printed in the French *Dictionary of Catholic Theology*. His earlier version read, "Although no explicit assertion of Catholic theology exists to corroborate this interpretation, it seems that we can logically draw the conclusion this far" — i.e., that in dignity St. Joseph surpasses not only the saints but all angels as well.[20]

To decide whether or not the Saint is truly so eminent, we can apply to St. Joseph the same principle Thomas Aquinas applied to Mary. "The Mother of God was superior to the angels with reference to the dignity to which she was divinely elevated. However, insofar as her state in the present life was concerned, she was inferior."[21] We reflect that the ministry of angels is to guard men; but the ministry of Joseph was to guard Jesus. Again, the guardianship of the angels even with respect to Jesus (as when "angels came and ministered to Him") (Mt. 4:11) is by no means as intimate as was St. Joseph's. Such ministry did not put the angels into the order of the hypostatic union. Hence, the dignity of exercising a true fatherhood of Jesus would seem to give St. Joseph an excellence far surpassing that of the angels.

St. Paul argues that the natural fatherhood of God the Father over God the Son makes Him "so much superior to the angels as He has inherited a more excellent name than they. For to which of the angels has He ever said, 'Thou art my Son, this day I have begotten thee'?" (Hebr. 1:4.) Parallelwise and always with due restrictions, we can apply this text to St. Joseph. To which of the angels was it ever said, "Thou shalt call his name Jesus"? (Mt. 1:21.) In other words no angel ever had the paternal right of bestowing the name on the divine Child; no angel was legally considered the father of Jesus; no angel ever received the submission of the Son of God to his command.

On grounds such as these Cantera concludes, "What can we say of St. Joseph relative to the angels and celestial spirits? Does he also excel them in dignity and excellence? We can affirm it with no fear, since it is not repugnant theologically that the Saint was predestined in order and in rank above them all. This affirmation is not certain doctrine of the Church, but there are solid reasons that accredit and verify it." The angels exercise sublime and adorable ministries of obedience and of love with regard to the Word Incarnate. However, these angelic ministries and adorations are not as profound and special and directly concerned with Jesus as was the ministry of St. Joseph. Even more, the degree of dignity is measured by the degree of love which souls attain in this life. St. Joseph, Cantera believes, made such progress in the love of God because of his closeness to Jesus that he advanced far beyond all the angels in a degree of *holiness* that gave him an equally prominent degree of *excellence.*[22]

ST. JOSEPH AND ST. JOHN THE BAPTIST

The question of St. Joseph's pre-eminence, however, arises not so much in connection with the angels as with John the Baptist. The superior rank assigned in the liturgy to the name of John the Baptist does not imply any inferiority on the part of St. Joseph, for as Benedict XIV makes it clear, the order of names in the liturgy is not intended to define the degree of dignity or holiness of the saints.[23] The reason for difficulty lies in the interpretation of the words of Jesus. "Amen I say to you, that among those born of women there has not risen a greater than John the Baptist" (Mt. 11:11). Hence, it is the gospel text rather than the liturgical rank of the two names (e.g., in the Litany of the Saints) that must receive our attention.

This judgment concerning relative order in the liturgy is a far cry from the negative attitude of a Consultor of the Congregation of Sacred Rites (evidently Jerome Saccheri, O.P.) who in 1869 recommended that the petitions for the advancement of the Saint's name in the liturgy be refused on every count save one, and this because St. Joseph's pre-eminence was doubtful. At the time, it is true, Joseph had not

been declared Patron of the Universal Church, undoubtedly
the most momentous Church action in glorifying Joseph on
earth. Nor had St. Joseph been granted the high liturgical
honors later accorded him by St. Pius X and Benedict XV.
Perhaps this might help explain the reluctance to champion
Joseph's dignity.

At any rate the Consultor of 1869 writes in evident sympathy with the action of Benedict XIII, who in 1726 felt that
Joseph's name should be placed in the Litany of the Saints,
but not before that of John the Baptist — "because to prefer
St. Joseph to the Precursor would have meant more excellent holiness and dignity in Joseph, something which cannot
be considered certain and evident; for the authority of the
Word of God, written or handed down, is not extant; and
there is also lacking any sort of tradition in the Catholic
Church.

"In this connection," the Consultor continues, "Suarez
himself, who first taught that St. Joseph obtained more
perfect grace than St. John the Baptist, adds that he holds
this as only probable. For the opposite opinion the saying
of Christ our Lord argues greater holiness and excellence in
St. John the Baptist: 'Amen I say to you, that among those
born of women there has not risen a greater than John the
Baptist' (Mt. 11:11), although this phrase receives different
interpretations."[24]

Such a view, of course, was entirely legitimate for its
author to hold since he considered his reasons theologically
sound. Particularly in this case where the Church has made
no definite and binding pronouncement free discussion has
been of great benefit for the cause of St. Joseph. As to the
assertions that "the authority of the Word of God, written or
handed down, is not extant," and as to the denial of any
Church tradition of Joseph's excellence, a few words of
recapitulation will suffice.

In the first place no competent writer would claim that
the explicit veneration of St. Joseph existed publicly from

the beginnings of the Church. But the *foundation* for attributing to the Saint his exclusive dignity and holiness is certainly found in the gospel narrative, and this is enough. Emphasis on St. Joseph's position and the fuller appreciation of it appeared relatively late in Church history.

Concerning the oft-cited text about John the Baptist, many comments are in order whose force and logic cannot be gainsaid. In fact, when our Lord declared that "among those born of women there has not risen a greater," He evidently did not expect His words to have a slavishly literal interpretation. Certain exceptions were to be made — at least He Himself and His mother Mary were not to be considered. Otherwise, Jesus as well as Mary would have been included in the number of "those born of women" as inferior to the Baptist. Clearly, then, exceptions to this statement of Jesus are justified if the dignity and holiness of the persons in question are manifest from some other source. If Joseph's pre-eminence cannot be reasonably denied, he too is to be exempt from the limitation that might at first sight seem to exist in our Lord's words.

In interpreting the Gospels it is a generally accepted principle that whenever doubt exists concerning a particular passage, the parallel description in another evangelist should be consulted, provided such a passage exists. In this instance Luke offers a more detailed report of Christ's language: "Among those born of women, there is not *a greater prophet* than John the Baptist" (Lk. 7:28). In other words, Luke's account shows that Jesus praised the Baptist as superior to all the prophets of the Old Testament.

This interpretation follows not only from the text but also from the context of both Matthew and Luke. Immediately after saying: "There has not risen a greater (prophet) than John the Baptist," Jesus adds (according to Matthew), "yet the least in the kingdom of *heaven* is greater than he," and (according to Luke), "yet the least in the kingdom of *God* is greater than he." Thereby all reasonable cause for difficulty is removed. The evangelists according to their wont give a substantial narrative, not repeated slavishly word for word, and they also make evident the hyperbolic language which Jesus used. Christ our Lord is indicating that the least ministry of the New Testament (which is truly the kingdom of heaven and the kingdom of God) is in itself far greater than the greatest ministry of the Old Testament, even as John the Baptist had fulfilled it.

Suarez helpfully points out that Joseph belongs neither properly nor exclusively to the Old and New Testaments.[25] Even more, Joseph's was the personal service of Christ in His hidden life, not a ministerial or a preaching activity such as that of the Apostles and their successors, the bishops of the Church.

The interpretation given here is confirmed by reliable authorities. Lagrange states, "Once again must we state that there is no question here of the personal holiness of the Baptist, but rather of his historical situation; he pertained to the law like others; he surpassed them by announcing the new order, but he is inferior to the workers of the king."[26] Cornelius a Lapide gives the theological reason for Joseph's superior dignity: "It is more to be father and ruler of Christ than to be His herald and forerunner."[27] Finally, Jones explains in *A Catholic Commentary on Holy Scripture*, "The Baptist is praised not so much for his personal sanctity as for the part he has so faithfully played in the divine scheme. . . . That John worthily fulfilled the function is supposed throughout, but our Lord is not speaking of his sanctity; it would be idle, therefore, to introduce the question, e.g., of our Lady's excelling sanctity in connection with the text. Yet (still in the order of dignity and not of sanctity) the members of the Kingdom (already in existence on earth) are more highly privileged."[28]

Certainly, then, John the Baptist was the greatest of the prophets. He had the gift of prophecy as well as the privilege of baptizing the Saviour. He alone fulfilled among all the prophets what the rest had prophesied. But for all his holiness and excellence, his closeness to Jesus and the dignity of his ministry must yield to St. Joseph's position as virginal husband of Mary, virgin father of Jesus, head of the Holy Family, and Patron of the Universal Church.

ST. JOSEPH AND THE APOSTLES

Another difficulty against St. Joseph's pre-eminence can arise when the vocation of the Saint is compared with that of the Apostles. The praise of the Apostles is explicitly set forth by Thomas Aquinas. Commenting on the text of St. Paul, "This grace has abounded beyond measure in us" (Eph. 1:8), St. Thomas writes, "From this there is manifest the rashness, not to say the error of those who presume to compare certain saints to the apostles in grace and glory; for it is clear from these words that the apostles have a greater grace than other saints, after Christ and the Virgin Mother."[29]

There are several answers to the difficulty proposed by St. Thomas. The words of St. Paul, "This grace has abounded beyond measure in us," do not have to be understood (as Aquinas understands them) in a comparison between the Apostles and the rest of the faithful. Hence, they do not necessarily imply that the Apostles would have more dignity than all other human beings except our Lady. They can be taken simply to mean that "we" — all the faithful — "are engulfed by the treasures of God's grace."[30]

Nevertheless, even if one does adopt St. Thomas' interpretation, there is still no real difficulty against St. Joseph's surpassing the Apostles in dignity. Joseph was dead at the time Paul was writing his supposed comparison; so was John the Baptist. Paul would have been speaking of those who were living. Francis Suarez answers the difficulty by remarking that the ministries of Joseph and of the Apostles cannot, properly speaking, be compared. Joseph's ministry concerns the order of the hypostatic union, and is in an essentially higher order than the ministry of the Apostles. Moreover, while the Apostles might be considered the greatest in the New Testament, Joseph belongs neither to the Old nor to the New Testament, but to the "Author and Cornerstone" of each.[31]

Michel comments, "It is incontestable that in the Middle Ages Joseph's cultus was hardly existent; the humble and modest saint was not thought of. . . . There is no question of a comparison of the apostles with a saint who came before them. . . ." He labels the whole objection from St. Paul's text and Thomas Aquinas' commentary on it as "a difficulty which in fact does not exist."[32]

REFERENCES — CHAPTER TWO

1. Aquinas, *ST*, 2a 2ae, q. 162, a. 4, c.
2. Aquinas, *ST*, 3, q. 27, a. 4, c.
3. Cf. *L'Ami du Clergé*, 38 (1921), 101, referring to Terrien, *La Mère de Dieu*, Paris, 1902, III, c. 2, t. 1, 259.
4. Aquinas, *ST*, 3, q. 27, a. 5, c.
5. This quotation is found in Suarez, "De Mysteriis Vitae Christi," disp. 8, and is attributed by him to Damascene. However, the *Oratio 3 de Nativ. Vir. Mariae*, its source, is not in the Migne Greek patrology. Romualdo Galdos, S.J., *Suarez Vulgarizado*, Granada, 1917, 6, locates it in the Paris edition of 1628 (383, 1°) of Damascene's works, noting that the phrase "by the singular gift of God" is not included.
6. *MNC*, 171.
7. *Ibid.*
8. Mueller, *Der heilige Joseph*, 184.
9. *Ibid.*, 181.
10. *Ibid.*, 185–188.
11. For an explanation of the incorrectness of "adoptive father," cf. *JJ*, 155.
12. Mueller, 186.
13. Prayers before Mass, *Roman Missal*.
14. *MNC*, 172.
15. *JJ*, 96.
16. Suarez, Disp. 8, sect. 1, n. 10.
17. *MNC*, 172.
18. *Ibid.*, 171.
19. Michel, *DTC*, 8, 1516, n. 2.
20. Cf. *L'Ami du Clergé*, 38 (1921), 105. This article is anonymous, but the article on St. Joseph in *DTC*, 8, 1510 ff. follows it almost verbatim; hence, the authorship must be the same.
21. Aquinas, *ST*, 3, q. 30, a. 2, ad 1.
22. Cantera, 340–342.

23. Benedict XIV, *De Beatificatione Servorum Dei et Canonizatione Beatorum*, Venice, 1767, 4, 2, c. 11, n. 20.

24. *Analecta Juris Pontificii*, Series 20 (1881), 842. This text was printed in Rome in 1869 in a 34-page pamphlet under the title, *Votum P. Fr. Hieronymi Pii Saccheri, O.P., S.R.C. Consultoris circa quatuor petitiones.*

25. Suarez, Disp. 8, sect. 1, n. 10.

26. M. J. Lagrange, O.P., *Evangile selon S. Luc*, Paris, 1925, 221.

27. Cornelius a Lapide, *Comm. in Matth.* 1:16 (*Commentaria in Scripturam Sacram* [Paris: Vivès, 1862], 15, 58).

28. A. Jones in *A Catholic Commentary on Holy Scripture*, ed. Orchard, Nelson, London, 1953, 871 (par. 694d-f).

29. Aquinas, *Comm. in Ep. ad Eph.* c. 1, lect. 3.

30. Cf. D. J. Leahy in *A Catholic Commentary on Holy Scripture*, 1121 (par. 899b); Kleist-Lilly, *The New Testament* (Milwaukee: Bruce), 487, "with this grace He has inundated us," Knox, *The New Testament* (New York: Sheed and Ward), 409, "so rich is God's grace that has overflowed upon us."

31. Suarez, Disp. 8, sect. 1, n. 10.

32. Michel, *DTC*, 8, 1515, n. 2.

CHAPTER THREE

St. Joseph's Holiness

THE doctrine that St. Joseph surpasses all creatures except Mary in holiness is becoming more and more commonly accepted in the Church. Some theologians have hesitated on the question whether the Saint surpasses the angels as well as all men, but their hesitation is admittedly due to a prudent reserve rather than a cognizance of facts that would permanently militate against St. Joseph.[1] This growth of the doctrine of the Saint's holiness does not of course involve any change in essential Catholic doctrine. Instead, there is question of a progressively deeper understanding of the significance of Joseph's vocation as virginal husband of Mary and virgin father of Jesus. Among modern authors who have written on St. Joseph's holiness the treatment is strikingly similar and at times almost identical.[2] The reason for this similarity is probably the same as existed with regard to St. Joseph's dignity — the existence of a common theological source, Francis Suarez. We shall summarize this traditional presentation here, amplifying it (as we did in the case of Joseph's dignity) with newer deductions drawn from St. Joseph's patronage of the Universal Church.

The connection between Joseph's dignity and Joseph's holiness is so close that at times the same wording can be used for the one as for the other. The two depend on each other as means to the end or as cause and effect. Joseph's dignity required that he be proportionately holy; Joseph's holiness grew out of the fact that the Saint possessed such dignity.

What is meant by holiness? It refers to freedom from all that is evil, to a supernatural likeness to God, and to the possession of sanctifying grace. More particularly, as heroic virtue, holiness represents the living picture of evangelical perfection: perfect purity from sin, intimate union with God, all ruled by the supreme norm of rightness.[3]

The Gospel of St. Matthew gives explicit testimony to Joseph's holiness when it calls him a just man (Mt. 1:19), or "right-minded."[4] The narrative of his life reveals his magnificent character even more pointedly. Among the great virtues he manifested are his unwavering faith, deep humility, consummate prudence, virginal chastity, and instant obedience. These are the effects appearing on the surface, as it were, that connote an underlying love of God which brings the Saint to a high order of sanctity. Of course, Joseph's virtues generally were not singled out for special mention in the early centuries of the Church. In the designs of God his position was obscure. While many of the Fathers gave lengthy tributes to the virtue of Joseph of Egypt, it is hard for us to understand at this distance why they passed over the humble foster father in silence. Even Augustine, who brilliantly analyzed Joseph's marriage and fatherhood, did not advance to the apparently logical step of eulogizing Joseph's holiness.

The only gospel text that drew notable comment on Joseph's virtues among the Fathers was the reference to the "just man" in Matthew. St. John Chrysostom's interpretation of the words is pioneering for its insight and rare for its length. His words of praise are still more unusual because in his opinion the espousal of Joseph and Mary was not a true marriage, and Mary supposedly was separated from Joseph on Calvary while Joseph was still living.[5] None the less, Chrysostom's tribute to the faith, magnanimity, and justice of St. Joseph is unsurpassed by any other tribute to the

Saint during the first millennium of the Church. That is why this long passage merits full inclusion here.

"'Joseph, her husband, being a just man.' Here, 'just man' means adorned with every virtue, for it pertains to justice not to be avaricious, and justice is the universal virtue. 'Being a just man,' that is, kind and self-controlled, he wished to dismiss her privately. Not only was he reluctant to punish Mary; he would not even deliver her up. Have you ever seen anyone who so loves wisdom and who is free from all tyrannical bent? He was so immune to [jealousy], this plague of the soul, that he refused to inflict pain on the Virgin even in the slightest degree.

"Accordingly, since it seemed that by law he was no longer permitted to keep her, and since it appeared that to denounce her and to bring her to trial was of necessity to put her to death, he chose neither course but began to elevate himself above the law. For with the coming of grace many prophetic types of this sublime institution were to appear. Just as the sun, not yet showing its rays, nevertheless illumines the zenith of the celestial vault from on high, so did Christ, who was about to emerge from the womb, illumine the whole world before His actual appearance." In this instance, Chrysostom says, such foreshadowing occurred through St. Joseph.

"Do you perceive the moderation of this man? He did not chastise, he mentioned the affair to no one, not even to her who was under suspicion, but he debated the matter within himself, seeking to hide from the Virgin the reason for separation. Nor does it say that he wished to cast her off, but rather to send her away, so kind and self-controlled was he.

"While he was pondering over all this, the angel appeared to him in sleep. Why not openly, in the manner that he appeared to the shepherds and to Zachary, as well as to the Virgin? This man was so ready to believe that he did not require such a manifestation. After Mary's conceiving, an evil suspicion took hold of his soul, but none the less he was ready to be easily led to good hope if only some one might come to lead him. Then it was that he received the revelation."

When the angel appears to Joseph, commanding him to flee into Egypt at once, Chrysostom comments, "Have you ever beheld such obedience, a soul so docile? Have you ever seen a spirit so alert, subject to no prejudice against anyone? When he suspected evil [of Mary], he was unwilling to keep her with him; but on the other hand, when such suspicion was removed, he no longer insisted on putting her away. Nay more: he kept her with himself, and he became a servant of this entire economy.

"When Joseph heard this message, he was not offended nor did he say, 'Here indeed is something very puzzling! You told me but recently, "He shall save his people" (Mt. 1:21); and now He is unable to save Himself, and we must flee on a long journey and change of place? This is contrary to your promise.' No, he uttered nothing of this sort, for he was a man of faith. Nor did he inquire the time of the return even though the angel spoke vaguely, saying, 'Remain there until I tell thee.' Thus, Joseph did not become slothful, but he obeyed and bent his will, and he bore all his trials with joy."[6]

This is certainly a keen analysis of Joseph's virtue drawn from the main events in Joseph's life. It shows how the gospel account indicates his holiness. However, from the mere analysis of his actions we would not be justified in claiming for him a holiness that surpasses all others except the holiness of Mary. So exceptional a claim can be made only indirectly by deduction. Theological principles must be used to argue to the holiness that *had* to exist in the man who carried out the vocation assigned to the head of the Holy Family.

The fundamental principle used by theologians is that applied to the Blessed Virgin by Thomas Aquinas, which we already noted in the preceding chapter: "Those whom

God chooses for an office, He prepares and disposes in such a way that they become suited to it."[7] Bernardine of Siena shows how this principle is extended to St. Joseph.

"As a general rule, covering all special graces communicated to rational creatures, whenever divine Providence chooses someone for a special grace or an exalted position, He endows the person thus chosen with all the gifts necessary for him and for his office. This principle was eminently verified in St. Joseph, the foster father of Jesus Christ and the true spouse of the Queen of Heaven and Mistress of angels. He was chosen by the Father as the faithful fosterer and guardian of His principal treasures, that is, His Son and Joseph's spouse; and this duty Joseph performed with all fidelity."[8]

Bernardine reasoned to the pre-eminence of St. Joseph as the greatest of the patriarchs, but it remained for John Gerson, the chancellor of the University of Paris, to be the first to mention explicitly a holiness for Joseph that surpassed that of all other men and angels after Mary. Gerson made the claim in his sermon at the Council of Constance, September 8, 1416. Implicitly, he based his conclusions on the requirements of St. Joseph's vocation. According to Gerson, "Mary is raised by grace and by glory above the choirs of angels — a fact which I do not dare to deny about Joseph although I do not presume to affirm it. There were present in both of them the perfections of other irrational and rational, even angelic creatures in a sort of eminent manner. . . . A devout meditative soul discovers enough to be inspired to praise Mary and Joseph in every way by justly ascribing to them . . . all the glory that exists in other creatures, the angels included. . . . If indeed Jesus did not lie when He said, 'Where I am, there also shall my servant be' (Jn. 12:26), then that man seems to be closer to Him in heaven who on earth was found, after Mary, to be more intimate, more obedient, and more faithful."[9]

The reasoning of Gerson, Bernardine, and Aquinas follows

out the connection that exists between high dignity and high holiness:

1. It is an ordinary law of the supernatural life that God confers grace proportioned to the office for which a person is selected. In other words when God Himself chooses some-one for a certain task, and when He absolutely wishes His candidate to carry out that duty with all perfection (especially when the task is most special), He confers grace that is best suited to its execution.

2. This law applies more strictly according to the degree that the office or dignity approaches a divine Person.

3. It has its strongest binding force for a man directly entrusted with the essentials of salvation in order that they might be handed on to others.[10]

Sometimes, we know, disloyal men have occupied high spiritual offices, as in the case of Judas discussed in the earlier chapter; but no such lack of aptitude occurs in those whom God has chosen efficaciously, foreseeing their signal co-opera-tion in the work of the Redemption. Always excepting Mary, no human being or angel was ever lifted to an office even equal to that of St. Joseph. Joseph's vocation brought him into most intimate contact with a divine Person. God did not so much commit to Joseph the grace necessary for the salvation of others; He confided to Joseph the very Author of salvation, the Source of all grace. Joseph was to protect our Lord's reputation, to provide Him with the necessities of life, to guard and rear Him to the full stature of His man-hood, to keep the secret of the Incarnation intact, to love Jesus as a father loves his God-given son. And if Joseph was prepared by God to exercise the authority of a father over Jesus, he must also have been prepared to be the holy hus-band and guardian of the Blessed Virgin. Otherwise, God would have failed to provide sufficiently for the holiness of Mary. It would have been most unseemly for Mary to share the intimacy of her family life with a sinner. Therefore, since no other person was ever so closely joined to Mary as was St. Joseph, his sanctity must have been as exclusive as was his vocation.

These different considerations are not necessarily separate and distinct proofs of the pre-eminent holiness of St. Joseph. They coalesce among themselves, confirm each other, or else show different aspects of Joseph's sanctity. They lead, for example, to another theological principle showing the connection between Joseph's dignity and sanctity. St. Thomas applied it to Mary; we extend it to demonstrate Joseph's close resemblance to Jesus and to Mary.

"To the degree that something approaches its source, by so much does it more participate in the effect of that source. Christ is the source of grace. The Blessed Virgin Mary was the closest to Christ in His humanity, because He took His human nature of her. Hence, in preference to all other people she had to receive the fulness of grace from Christ."[11] But, always with the exception of our Lady, no one approached Christ, the source of grace, more closely than did St. Joseph. *Joseph's intimacy with Jesus was never equaled.* He was in Christ's presence for all the long years of the Hidden Life, and he merited even to "carry, to kiss, to clothe and protect Him."[12] The holiness that befitted Joseph should, therefore, have been second to the holiness of Mary.

Yet, even more, we recall that if Joseph was close to our Lord, he was also close to our Lady. His was the privileged proximity to Mary, the mediatrix and aqueduct of all graces. Through Mary, Joseph would be assured of receiving the richest inspirations of grace to attain sterling holiness. Mary could not fail to pray for her virginal husband, to whom she owed so much for his selfless affectionate service. As phrased by Bernardine of Siena, "Because the Virgin knew how great was the unity of marriage in its spiritual love, she also knew that Joseph had been given her by the Holy Spirit as her spouse and as a trustworthy guardian of her virginity, to share her love and her service of the divine Son of God. This is why I believe that she loved St. Joseph most sincerely with all her heart."[13]

Suarez takes up the same idea in greater detail. "It is likely that the Blessed Virgin asked for and obtained by her prayers precious gifts and helps of grace for her spouse, whom she loved with singular devotion. For if it is true, as indeed it is, that one of the most efficacious means of obtaining grace from God is devotion to the Blessed Virgin, who cannot believe that most holy Joseph, beloved of the Virgin and most devoted to her, received utmost perfection of holiness? . . . It is part of a wife's virtue and sanctity that she love her husband and desire and procure for him every benefit, especially for his soul. The Blessed Virgin was all-perfect in everything; hence, she excelled in this love as well. Moreover, we should consider the gratitude which is owed to one's benefactors and which is better repaid by nothing except love. St. Joseph suffered much, and he endured many labors because of the Virgin, all with a manifestly unique, generous, and willing love."[14]

As with the love of Mary for Joseph, so with the love of Jesus for Joseph. Christ's love for His parents was that of a grateful, devoted son. We logically conclude that after Mary no creature except Joseph held so high a place in the affections of our Lord. For His father on earth His was the love of the most perfect of sons, a love tendered to the man who acted in the stead, as it were, of the eternal Father in heaven. Jesus would have been negligent in His filial duties if He had failed to procure the spiritual welfare of St. Joseph. We cannot doubt the exceptional reward Jesus would intend for the Saint because of so many works of paternal love.

Finally, we arrive at indications of St. Joseph's holiness from the fact that no natural force is more powerful than example. Proverbially, the simple truth has been expressed that "words exercise influence, but example draws one in its wake." Only Mary and Joseph lived for so long a time in the intimate company of God made man, and only Joseph daily beheld the joint example of Jesus and Mary — God Himself, and God's most perfect creature. Bernardine of Siena expresses the idea thus: "If we wretches often can make progress by living with holy men who, compared to the Virgin, are nothing, what tremendous progress should we not attribute to Joseph, who lived with the Virgin! How much perfection must have accrued to him by living with God, blessed Jesus!"[15] And in our own day we try to appreciate the sanctifying power of receiving Jesus in the Blessed Sacrament and in praying to Him in His sacramental bodily presence. Joseph lived in that physical presence of Jesus not for a few moments or days but constantly during the Hidden Life. The holy house at Nazareth was the tabernacle, and Joseph like Mary cradled the child Jesus in the ciborium of his arms.

St. Joseph's patronage of the Universal Church can be taken as another indication of his exceptional holiness even though in a certain sense this is not an independent norm. The patronage of the Church is an extension of Joseph's care of the Holy Family; and Joseph's holiness has already been deduced from the requirements of his Holy Family vocation. Nevertheless, the patronage, even if not completely distinct, acts as a sort of corollary. According to St. Thomas the more perfect love the saints possess in heaven, by so much more do they pray for men and to such a degree can they help us.[16] In other words, the more close their union with God, by so much is their efficacy as patron saints increased.

We can apply these principles to St. Joseph conversely. In his case by the inspiration of the Holy Spirit he has been officially declared Patron of the Church, for everyone, everywhere. Therefore, his fatherly protection is extended over all, and the Church has entrusted itself to his loving care. No other saint has ever been given such a tribute. St. Michael is a sort of military protector of the Church, not its patron; all other saints are at best diocesan or local or class patrons. Joseph, however, because he is the Patron of the *entire —*

"universal," "catholic" — Church, must equivalently be patron for *all,* and therefore *in all things.*

In Michel's words, "A role no less glorious has followed
upon Joseph's part in the Incarnation, now completed — that
of protector of the Church, this Church which continues the
mystery of the Incarnation on earth. If Jesus Christ as head
of the Church must have the fulness of grace which belongs
to the head, a 'fulness of which we have all received' — if the
holy Virgin, insofar as she is mother of men must possess a
grace more perfect than that of other creatures — can we not
equally affirm that the role of protector of the Church consti-
tutes for St. Joseph a title to an exceptional" — and, we would
add, a strictly unique — "superabundance of grace"?[17] Thus
it is that St. Joseph as husband, as father, as head of the
household, and as universal patron evidently must be gifted
with a likeness to God similar though inferior to Mary's. The
writings of recent popes concerning this holiness show forth
the mind of the Church. The documents implicitly repeat
the theological principle, "Holiness must befit such dignity;
such dignity requires parallel holiness."

Benedict XV says, "How numerous and how exalted were
the virtues with which he adorned his poor and humble con-
dition! And among all these virtues *none was wanting* to
ennoble the man who was to be the husband of Mary Immaculate and who was to be thought the father of our Lord
Jesus Christ."[18]

In 1870 when Pius IX proclaimed the Saint as Patron of
the Universal Church, he referred to him as "another Joseph,
of whom the first Joseph had been the type." The holiness of
Joseph of Egypt is clearly described by Scripture. But if
Joseph of Egypt is but a type of Joseph of Nazareth, evidently
the holiness of the virgin father is much greater. Pius IX also
adopted the words of St. Bernard regarding Joseph's exclusive intimacy with Jesus, paraphrasing them as "And so it
was that Him, whom countless kings and prophets had of old
desired to see, Joseph not only saw but conversed with, and

embraced in paternal affection, and kissed, and most sed-
ulously nourished." And *"because* of this sublime dignity
which God conferred on His most faithful servant" — an
intimation that Joseph's dignity must imply commensurate
holiness? — "the Church has always most highly honored and
praised blessed Joseph next to his spouse, the Virgin Mother
of God."[19] The Church would not single out any saint so
extraordinarily unless his holiness was equally extraordinary
and would call for imitation.

The idea of Joseph's supernatural fitness for his vocation
always recurs. Pius IX begins his liturgical decree of 1871
with the words, "The Catholic Church rightly honors *with
its highest cultus* and venerates with a feeling of deep
reverence the illustrious patriarch blessed Joseph, now
crowned in glory and honor in heaven, whom Almighty God
in preference to all His saints willed to be the chaste and
true spouse of the Immaculate Virgin Mary as well as the
putative father of His only-begotten Son. He enriched him
and *filled him to overflowing with entirely unique graces* in
order that he might execute most faithfully the duties of so
sublime a state."[20]

The most explicit teaching of the Church is the classic,
oft-repeated passage of Leo XIII in *Quamquam Pluries.*
Joseph "indeed was the husband of Mary and the father, as
was supposed, of Jesus Christ. From *this* arise *all* his dignity,
grace, *holiness,* and glory. . . . There can be no doubt that
more than any other person he approached that supereminent
dignity by which the Mother of God is raised far above all
created natures. . . . Joseph *alone* stands out in august dignity
because he was the guardian of the Son of God by the divine
appointment."[21] When we commented earlier on this passage,
we noted that Leo deduces Joseph's dignity and holiness
from Joseph's double vocation; but, he adds, in *dignity*
Joseph is second only to Mary. Logically the inference is
justified that in *holiness,* too, Joseph is second only to Mary.

The encyclical explicitly mentions some of the virtues

Joseph exercised according to the gospel narrative. Later in the encyclical, Pope Leo points out at even greater length why Joseph is so universal a patron for all classes of people: he possesses virtues which all can imitate.[22] This is the theme to which the pope returns in his letter on the Holy Family. Here is the picture of Joseph as uniquely holy, and therefore patron for all, because in the Holy Family "all men were to behold the perfect exemplar of domestic virtues as well as of all virtue and holiness. . . . We cannot doubt that all the glories of domestic life, taking their origin in mutual love, saintly character, and the exercise of piety were *without exception* manifested in a superlative degree by the Holy Family, as a pattern for all other families to imitate. To this end, a benign Providence had established the Holy Family, in order that all Christians in whatever walk of life or situation might have a reason and an incentive to practice every virtue, provided they would fix their gaze on the Holy Family. In Joseph, therefore, heads of the household are blessed with the unsurpassed model of fatherly watchfulness and care."[23] We should note in these words how "all virtue" is to be found "without exception" and "in a superlative degree" in the Holy Family. Joseph's rank in this family automatically would indicate that his holiness is above the holiness of all others outside it.

To crown these tributes the Church has given St. Joseph certain exclusive honors which he shares with our Blessed Lady alone — among them, a special litany, a proper preface in the Mass, and an invocation in the Divine Praises. The Litany of St. Joseph is a prolonged tribute to Joseph's sanctity. In it he is invoked as exercising particular virtues in an outstanding degree: justice, chastity, prudence, bravery, obedience, and faith; and his patronage indicates further virtues of his life: patience, poverty of spirit, industriousness, family care, protection against sin, sympathy for the afflicted and dying, hatred of the devil, and stanch guardianship of the Church.[24] Of course, it is true that liturgical rank does not *of itself* indicate the Church's belief in a saint's holiness, greater or less. None the less, because these ritual privileges are not isolated, they seem to show that the Church sets Joseph's patronage second to that of our Lady. We recall that a more extensive patronage grows out of correspondingly greater holiness of the patron saint.

In understanding this analysis of the gifts showered on St. Joseph to make him holy and worthy of his vocation, one final caution is needed. We must not think that such sanctity was strictly passive. God had foreseen from all eternity the co-operation of the Saint. The divine choice of St. Joseph gives us a hint of the degree of Joseph's self-immolation. Mary is the Queen of Martyrs, and the holiest of human beings and angels. If Joseph is second only to Mary in sanctity, then he likewise must be second only to her in putting to death any will of his own that might resist the will of eternal Love. St. Francis de Sales gives him this tribute: "Although it is true that Mary possessed every virtue in a higher degree than is attainable by any other pure creature, yet it is quite certain that the glorious St. Joseph was the being who approached most nearly to that perfection. . . . All her virtues and perfections were absolutely reflected in St. Joseph, so that it almost seemed as if he were as perfect and possessed all virtues in as high a degree as did the glorious Virgin."[25]

REFERENCES — CHAPTER THREE

1. Cf. Reg. Garrigou-Lagrange in *La Vie Spirituelle*, 19 (1928), 662; Michel, *DTC*, 8, 1516, 2°.

2. As in Bover, Garrigou-Lagrange, Lépicier, Macabiau, Michel, Mueller, *passim;* summarily in Herrmann. (Cf. bibliography.)

3. Cantera, 345; cf. Aquinas, *ST*, 2a, 2ae, q. 81, art. 8.

4. As translated by Knox and by Kleist. Cf. Kleist-Lilly, *The New Testament*, 16.

5. John Chrysostom, *In Matth.* hom. 5, 3 (*MG* 57, 58).

6. *In Matth.* hom. 4, 3; 4, 5; 5, 3; 8, 3 (*MG* 57, 43–46; 57; 85).

7. Aquinas, *ST*, 3, q. 27, a. 4, c.

8. Bernardine of Siena, *Sermo de S. Joseph*, Introd. (*SI* 1, 2); for the literary dependence of Bernardine on Ubertino of Casale, who in *Arbor vitae*

crucifixae Jesu (1305) wrote much of the material Bernardine later used, cf. Joseph Dusserre, "Les Origines de la dévotion à saint Joseph," in *CJ*, 1 (1953), 186, and 2 (1954), 17.

9. John Gerson, Sermon of September 8, 1416, Exordium, Consid. 4 (*SI* 134, 133, 198).

10. Macabiau, 167–168.

11. Aquinas, *ST*, 3, q. 27, a. 5, c.

12. Bernard of Clairvaux, *Hom. 2 super Missus Est*, 16 (*ML* 183, 70).

13. Bernardine of Siena, *Sermo de S. Joseph*, art. 2, 1 (*SI* 17).

14. Suarez, Disp. 8, sec. 2, n. 1; sec. 1, n. 6.

15. Bernardine of Siena, *Sermo*, art. 2, 2 (*SI* 37).

16. Aquinas, *ST*, 2a, 2ae, q. 83, art. 11, resp.

17. A. Michel in *DTC*, 8, 1514; also in *L'Ami du Clergé*, 38 (1921), 102.

18. Benedict XV, *Bonum Sane, AAS*, 12, 313; tr. from *MNC*, 181.

19. Pius IX, *Quemadmodum Deus, ASS*, 6, 193; tr. from *MNC*, 163.

20. *Inclytum Patriarcham, ASS*, 6, 324; tr. from *MNC*, 165.

21. *MNC*, 171.

22. *MNC*, 173.

23. *Neminem Fugit*, Decr. No. 3777 of S.R.C.; tr. from *MNC*, 176–177.

24. *AAS*, 1, 290.

25. Francis de Sales, *The Spiritual Conferences*, tr. by Sisters of the Visitation (London: Burns, Oates, 1909), 368.

CHAPTER FOUR

St. Joseph's Privileges

IN NO other section of Josephite theology does so little explicit evidence exist as with regard to St. Joseph's privileges or prerogatives. Here more than anywhere else we must depend on the principle of deducing the Saint's prerogatives from the requirements of his office. This means that the answer to most of the questions to occur will have to be, "It is fitting," "It is only probable," or "We don't know."

Because of this one might fear that the discussion will defeat its purpose by overclouding truths that are well established. Trained theologians are properly equipped to explore new frontiers of knowledge by investigation and by argument. Yet what is helpful for experts can understandably become confusing, even dangerous for a general reader.

A caution such as this is prudent and valid. However, we believe that in the present case it does not apply. The interested reading public is not unacquainted with the fact that difficult and subtle issues developed in the past concerning St. Joseph. Once people read of the historical claims that have been made for the Saint, they themselves wish to learn the intrinsic grounds for such claims. They are not bettered by having a puzzling religious question deliberately left unanswered when legitimate inquiries can be settled with a decisive reply, even though (as in this chapter) the reply will usually be based only on probability.

Reduced to specific categories, the questions on the various

spiritual prerogatives of St. Joseph are actually details of his
holiness. They are concerned with his first acquisition of
sanctifying grace, with the conservation of grace during life,
and with the reward of grace after death. According to this
division, in the historical picture St. Joseph has been claimed
as conceived immaculate or purified of original sin in his
mother's womb. Writers and preachers have also speculated
on his freedom from sin throughout his career: was he preserved by God from mortal sin, from deliberate and semideliberate venial sin, and even from the temptations of
concupiscence? Finally, concerning his lot after death, did
his body rise from the dead so that at this very moment he
is in heaven, body and soul, like Jesus and Mary? These are
the subjects we shall discuss in this chapter, admittedly
among the most speculative topics of the theology of St.
Joseph.

One guiding principle should be kept in mind. We would
not be justified in departing from the teaching of Leo XIII
that St. Joseph became a unique sharer in Mary's dignity
and holiness by reason of his marriage. His position as
virginal husband of the Mother of God and even more his
position as virgin father of Jesus Christ required a worthy
subject, who in God's plans received a fitting preparation
and a fitting reward. But to what extent did Joseph's holiness
resemble that of Mary? In other words how far may (and
should) Mary's privileges of grace be extended to her spouse?

The grace under discussion is what theologians call *gratum
faciens,* that is, grace which "makes a soul pleasing" to God.
This is the grace which justifies and sanctifies the individual, and brings about union with God. There is another
type of grace called *gratis data* — "freely given," "gratuitous"
— which is directed not so much to the sanctification of the
person who possesses it but is rather ordained to sanctify
others. Graces of this second type are, for instance, the power
to work miracles, to speak in unknown tongues, to prophesy,
to read the secrets of hearts, and like gifts all of which have

the prime purpose of instructing others in faith and persuading them exteriorly. These are called charisms.

Sometimes the claim has been made that St. Joseph possessed such *gratiae gratis datae* in view of the fact that his holiness is so exalted. But such a claim is not valid. To estimate these graces for working miracles and similar marvels, we must realize that these gifts do not suppose holiness in their owner, and it can even be that a person in sin receives them from God. For the one who has such charismatic gifts, they do not cause holiness either effectively or meritoriously although in many cases they accompany holiness. We cannot judge the saints' love for God by any such extraordinary phenomena. Hence, with regard to St. Joseph we should say that Joseph had none of them unless perchance they were necessary for his double vocation in the Holy Family. The Saint's mission was not to teach others. Graces which the Apostles required in their ministry were useless for Joseph. Therefore, as Cardinal Gotti concludes, "In those graces which particularly belonged to his ministry, Joseph surpassed all other men; in other gifts and graces, he could be surpassed by others."[1]

Cantera's analysis is worth noting here. Having chosen Joseph to co-operate in the mystery of the Incarnation, he writes, the Lord filled him with abundant and special graces, outstanding prerogatives that were in agreement with the exalted destiny to which he was predestined. But it is a reprehensible extreme to infer that Joseph was given all the charisms (i.e., miraculous gifts) which God bestowed on all Christian saints. Such a bestowal is not linked with greater or lesser holiness of soul; it has a special evangelistic and apostolic purpose. Consequently, we do not have a right to claim for St. Joseph all the privileges of other saints simply because he was the greatest of the saints after Mary. We must admit always, however, that those graces belong to him which he needed with respect to his office. "We must always travel on the path traversed by our predecessors, not departing from the sources of revelation as legitimately interpreted by the authority of the Church or by the principles of solid theological reasoning."[2]

AN IMMACULATE CONCEPTION?

During the late Middle Ages, when the devotion to St. Joseph was coming to the fore, certain overzealous proponents defended what they called an "immaculate conception" of St. Joseph. In some of these cases it seems that the real meaning of the term was clouded over or altogether misunderstood in the minds of these writers and preachers. One would judge that they were rather arguing for a prenatal sanctification of the Saint after he (like all other humans except Mary) had contracted original sin, the debt of Adam.

In succeeding centuries a small number of authors actually claimed for St. Joseph the identical privilege granted our Blessed Lady. In our own day the opinion was resurrected by José D. M. Corbató, who in 1907 asserted that Joseph like Mary possessed sanctifying grace from the first moment of his existence. Corbató's book was promptly placed on the Index of Forbidden Books. However, we cannot automatically reject his doctrine about Joseph's "immaculate conception" merely because of this prohibition by the Church. His book was suppressed, according to the decree, "especially" for a different reason. He had proposed and defended "a divine fatherhood of St. Joseph in the real and proper sense of the word."[3]

Practically all of the quotations brought forward by Corbató to support his opinion did not actually affirm Joseph's immaculate conception. At best the texts spoke of Joseph's great holiness in general, his purity of life, and his exalted dignity. They did not descend to concrete privileges, and the few claims made for such a doctrine were from panegyric sermons, not from the writings of Catholic theologians.

An argument that might have weight in deducing the privilege for Joseph is the reasoning based on the law of nature governing the likeness of husband and wife. Such likeness, it has been said, should be in qualities of soul as well as of body. Accordingly, since the Blessed Virgin was conceived without original sin, the same privilege belonged to him who was made worthy to be her virginal husband.[4]

This line of reasoning fails in its fundamental point. The absolute spiritual likeness that is postulated for husband and wife is in reality not required. Moreover, any such likeness would have to exist only during the years of marriage, if this argument held. Far more cogent than such a principle is the probative value of the doctrine of original sin. St. Paul states that all men sinned in Adam (Rom. 5:12). This rule is so universal that no one has the right to invoke exceptions to it without the strongest reasons for doing so. In the case of our Lady the tradition of the Church has vindicated the highest privileges for her from the infant years of the Church. When the Council of Trent officially and explicitly defined the universal extent of original sin, it mentioned at the same time that it did not intend to include the Blessed Virgin in its decree.[5] No other exception was made. Finally, in the Bull of Pius IX defining the Immaculate Conception of our Lady the Pope stated that this privilege belonged to her in a singular fashion.[6]

The retort has been made that the privilege would still remain "singular" if another person in addition to Mary received it; that the Bull defined the *privilege,* not the *exclusiveness* of the privilege; and that the mind of the Council of Trent was not to limit to Mary alone the exception from the definition on original sin.[7] Against this, the thought of the Church seems to be clearly expressed, so much so that of the theologians who have studied the pertinent documents and history, some (with Lepicier[8]) have not hesitated to call "rash and suspect of heresy" the opinion that St. Joseph was conceived without original sin in the same way as was our Lady. Other theologians place a slightly milder censure on the proposition, namely, that it is against the common and certain view of Catholic theology. In either case the agreement against it is practically unanimous. In Cantera's judgment, belief in the immaculate conception of St. Joseph could be an object of private belief but not of public faith. If an individual wished to satisfy private piety by privately attributing such a privilege to St. Joseph, that person would not sin; but to defend it theologically would be neither prudent nor secure. "The differences between Mary and Joseph are not in degree but in kind."[9]

St. Joseph would be the first to call attention to the all-special prerogative of his virginal wife. We affirm that Mary alone was conceived without original sin, to prepare her to become the Mother of God.

JOSEPH'S PRENATAL SANCTIFICATION?

We come now to the question concerning the sanctification of St. Joseph in the womb of his mother. This doctrine, like several others concerning the Saint, was first proposed by John Gerson in his sermon at the Council of Constance in 1416. Other pioneers of the devotion to St. Joseph also held the doctrine: Isidor de Isolanis, Bernardine of Busti, and Alphonsus Liguori.[10] Liguori makes the assertion that Suarez holds the view also, but Suarez actually refuses to take such a stand, or in fact any stand. He believes that since both Scripture and the official tradition of the Church are silent on the point, we do not have sufficient evidence to form a correct judgment.[11]

The outstanding reason for holding that Joseph was purified of original sin in the womb of his mother is one of fitness. It is proper, so the argument goes, that the man whom God chose to be the husband of the Blessed Virgin and the virgin father of Jesus should have been sanctified by a special privilege of God in a more excellent way than any other human being. The privilege of prenatal sanctification is attributed to John the Baptist by all theologians; and to other saints of the Old and New Testament by a certain number. Accordingly, by a stronger right the privilege must have been granted to St. Joseph, who was far more than merely a patriarch, prophet, or even forerunner of Christ. In the words of John of Carthagena, "Every sanctification in the womb was because of the unusual future dignity of the one sanctified, or because he had a relationship to Christ, the saint of saints, in a very special manner. Both facts are eminent in our Joseph; for he was the first whom the Holy Spirit canonized in the New Testament, calling him 'just'; and above all other men he bore a prior and immediate relationship toward Christ, to protect Him in His infancy."[12] Isidore de Isolani gives two reasons for Joseph's prenatal sanctification: Jeremias and John the Baptist were thus sanctified — *a fortiori* the privilege must have been granted to Joseph. And if the dignity of her Son led to Mary's Immaculate Conception, then Joseph's dignity must have led to his sanctification before his birth.[13]

The contrary arguments generally used against this privilege for St. Joseph are drawn from a principle stated by Thomas Aquinas. After St. Thomas sets forth his opinion that the prophet Jeremias as well as John the Baptist were sanctified in the wombs of their mothers, he adds, "Nor are we to believe that any others were sanctified in the womb, of whom Scripture makes no mention; for privileges of this sort, granted to some persons over and above the ordinary rule, are directed to the utility of others, according to the text, 'the manifestation of the Spirit is given to everyone for profit' (1 Cor. 12:7); but there would be no profit for the sanctification of others, arising from the sanctification of some in the womb, unless the Church would be made aware of the fact."[14]

The *a fortiori* comparison of St. Joseph with John the Baptist and the prophet Jeremias means little or nothing in probative value when we realize that sanctification in the womb does not necessarily indicate greater holiness. The argument shows even more weakness if we consider that almost every claim for sanctification of this sort has failed to receive common acceptance among theologians. "We are unable to say with certainty that anyone was sanctified in the womb except John the Baptist."[15]

Far from holding the sanctification of Jeremias in the womb of his mother, the contrary opinion is defended by a great number of Fathers, theologians, and exegetes.[16] Even though the words in Jeremias 1:5 have been translated as "Before thou emerged from the womb, I sanctified thee," the meaning of *sanctify* in the original Hebrew means "to be prepared" or "to be destined for something." This meaning is brought out, for example, in the Knox translation, "Before thou ever camest to the birth, I set thee apart for myself."[17]

Scripture certainly gives no hint of prenatal sanctification for St. Joseph; the Fathers of the Church make no such allusion; and the Church documents do not refer to it in any way. Hence, the negative opinion states that we do not have sufficient reason to defend Joseph's purification from original sin before his birth. It is no valid argument to claim that Joseph must have been sanctified in the womb because he was a just man. While it is true that Joseph's vocation required most extraordinary graces and freedom from actual sin, this still does not indicate any necessity for prenatal sanctification. The fact that John the Baptist received the privilege would not create in Joseph any deficiency in holiness with respect to St. John. At whatever time sanctifying grace was infused into Joseph's soul, that grace was already more abundant and more magnificent than the grace accorded any other creature with the exception of Mary. Benedict XIV, writing as a private theologian, plainly stated that the affirmative view for Joseph's sanctification before his birth "lacks a firm and stable foundation in sacred theology."[18]

Apparently we must conclude that for the present this

will remain an open question. The truth lies concealed in the mystery of the grandeur with which God has surrounded the Saint of the Hidden Life. No argument on either side seems final. We have no intrinsic evidence to decide against the belief; we have no certain evidence for it. To say that Joseph's sanctification was required only from the time he was espoused to Mary and not beforehand, fails to take into account God's preparation of the Saint for his vocation.

As for Thomas Aquinas' appeal to the lack of evidence — which is probably the strongest argument in favor of the negative view — it is noteworthy that Aquinas sets aside his own limitation when speaking of this same question with reference to our Lady. "Nothing is handed down in the canonical Scriptures concerning the sanctification of the Blessed Mary as to her being sanctified in the womb; indeed, they do not even mention her birth. But as Augustine in his tractate on the Assumption of the Virgin argues with reason, since her body was assumed into heaven, and yet Scripture does not relate this, so it may reasonably be argued that she was sanctified in the womb. For it is reasonable to believe that she who brought forth the 'only-begotten of the Father, full of grace and truth' (Jn. 1:14) received greater privileges of grace than all others. . . . Moreover, it is to be observed that it was granted by way of privilege to others to be sanctified in the womb. . . . It is therefore with reason that we believe the Blessed Virgin to have been sanctified before her birth from the womb."[19] Might it "reasonably be argued" that Joseph, too, was sanctified in the womb, even though the Scriptures do not relate this?

Demaret offers an original approach that other theologians seem to have overlooked. He denies the principle of St. Thomas, namely, that sanctification in the womb would be a charism, a grace primarily ordained for the sanctification of others rather than for the individual receiving it. It is instead, he says, intrinsically in the order of sanctifying grace, and it is ordained for the sanctification of St. Joseph. Its only unusual characteristic is the time of its bestowal, i.e., before Joseph's birth. None the less, it concerns the question of making St. Joseph an adopted son of God as soon as possible, thus preparing him as early as possible for the office which would later require in him holiness so exalted. If by theological deduction the fact of Joseph's prenatal sanctification becomes evident, then indeed this gift would be of value for the sanctification of others, and the Church would be made aware of the fact — both requirements laid down by St. Thomas.[20]

Our ultimate opinion comes close to that of Cornelius a Lapide. "God could have given this privilege to many people, but whether He actually did so, we do not know. By all means, if after the Blessed Virgin He bestowed it on any of those mentioned earlier, it seems that He did not deny it to St. Joseph her spouse."[21] Even so valiant a defender of St. Joseph speaks conditionally at best.

THE SINLESSNESS OF ST. JOSEPH

Concerning St. Joseph's sinlessness, various degrees or subdivisions can be considered.[22] In ascending order we can ask

1. Whether Joseph committed any mortal sin during his life, or was his soul so flooded with the riches of grace that he was strengthened against all grievous sin, retaining of course full exercise of his free will?

2. Whether he ever committed deliberate or semideliberate venial sin, or was he preserved by God's efficacious grace from doing so?

3. Whether a still higher privilege was bestowed on him, namely, the restraint of concupiscence?

To begin with, we must affirm without the slightest hesitation that the Saint was not impeccable. We use the word in this sense: the *possibility* of sin existed in Joseph's life. His could never be, for example, the sinlessness of Jesus, for whom it was impossible to violate the law of God because of the union of the human and the divine nature in the Second divine Person. We are concerned with the *fact*, rather than the *possibility* of Joseph's sinning, in so far as this fact or absence of fact can be deduced from theological reasoning. In other words, *did* St. Joseph ever commit actual sin? Or was he given such graces that the inclination to sin was restrained in him, and he was able to avoid not only mortal but also venial sin? On this subject dogmatic certitude either from Holy Scripture or from official Church teaching does not exist. It must be remembered that our findings are based on theological probability according to the evidence at hand.

All authorities agree that St. Joseph must have been confirmed in grace. This is a minimum opinion, generally accepted. It means that God's providence surrounded the Saint with such helps that he did not sin grievously nor, in general, did he commit fully deliberate sin. The reason usually given for holding this opinion rests on Joseph's vocation and on his intimacy with Mary and with Jesus.

According to Richard, after Joseph's virginal marriage to our Lady the Saint certainly did not sin in the matter of chastity; after the birth of our Lord he did not sin in any other aspect as well.[23] Hervé is more conservative. He believes that the doctrine of St. Joseph's sinlessness cannot be proved, and that the inclination to sin (concupiscence) was not restrained in the Saint. But St. Joseph was confirmed in grace at least from the time of the marriage because "at that time his mission began." For the avoidance of all venial sins after the marriage, Hervé continues, "This does not seem to be something that should be conceded; but it is conceded by many, that he avoided fully deliberate venial sins with regard to chastity."[24]

Michel also takes a strict stand. He writes, "Lepicier defends the thesis of sinlessness with much conviction, basing it upon the perfect purity which the mission of St. Joseph required. Our piety toward St. Joseph does not oblige us, it seems, to affirm this thesis without restriction. The mission of St. Joseph required sinlessness, but only in the time when the mission was confided to him." It is possible, Michel adds, that God accorded the privilege of sinlessness to Joseph throughout his whole life. Yet because such a great gift is so complete and so rare, we ought to require evidence that is much more convincing than that which is ordinarily brought forward. The Council of Trent defined that man cannot avoid sin without a special privilege from God.[25] This privilege was certainly conceded to Mary as a consequence of her Immaculate Conception. But while we recognize the possibility of so exceptional a gift being lavished on creatures other than our Lady, we must also recognize that the fact of its concession cannot be demonstrated by theological argument. "All that we have reason to affirm is that St. Joseph by reason of the mission confided to him was confirmed in grace from the instant of his marriage to the Blessed Virgin. Would it not be more exact simply to say that St. Joseph was constituted in grace in a pre-eminent manner (a privilege which does not necessarily imply sinlessness), and that from the first moment of his use of reason he did not cease increasing the superabundant treasure of sanctifying grace which God bestowed on him at that time?"[26]

Against this view is the reasoning of Cantera, Demaret, Llamera, Msgr. Sinibaldi, Cardinal Lepicier, and other theologians. This group not only holds that St. Joseph was free from mortal and venial sin during his entire life, but also that concupiscence was held in check in St. Joseph by God's special grace.

The "concupiscence" which will be discussed refers to the inordinate and indeliberate attraction of our sense nature toward its proper objects. As a result of the sin of Adam our body is no longer completely subject to the control of reason. We cannot govern our sense reactions so that they invariably agree with the dictates of reason. Even in the enjoyment of legitimate sense objects we often feel an inclination to press forward to an illicit degree; or perhaps the inclination arises to obtain a pleasure that is wholly wrong in itself. In either case this inclination is both *inde-liberate* (arising without or despite our desire) and *inordinate* (against the dictates of right reason obedient to God's laws). Because an act of concupiscence understood in this strict sense is indeliberate, in itself it is no sin. If conquered, it is an occasion to gain merit. But it can frequently lessen the fervor with which a good action is performed. In the words of the Council of Trent, "The Holy Synod declares that the Catholic Church never understood that this concupiscence which the Apostle sometimes calls sin (Rom. 6:12 ff) is called sin because it is truly and properly sin in those reborn, but because it is from sin, and it inclines to sin."[27]

Freedom from concupiscence can be defined as "The rectitude according to which the sensitive appetite is perfectly subordinated to reason, so that it in no way moves the will toward an object contrary to reason."[28] Such rectitude can occur either because the inclination to sin is restrained, or, what is greater, because it is totally removed or extinguished. The latter occurred in the case of our Lady, because the disorder of concupiscence is a sequel of original sin, and Mary was conceived without original sin. Hence, she never inherited the power and propensity which inclined to disordered movements.

But St. Joseph was not conceived without original sin. Therefore, such a *propensity* did exist in him, even though — in the present supposition — there occurred no *actual* sense movement anticipating and resisting the rule of reason. Llamera advises great care in making this claim for St. Joseph. "Authors are not lacking who, without making their words precise, repeat the phrase of Gerson, who said that the concupiscence might be completely *extinguished* at the moment of conception for one who did not contract original sin, as happened in the case of our Lady. It might be *ligated*, i.e., restrained by God's grace, as we claim in the case of St. Joseph, who did contract original sin and consequently also contracted the concupiscence that is the effect of sin."[29]

Here, then, is the exact question: Did the grace of God bring it about that St. Joseph never felt the sting and rebellion of concupiscence? We can argue only from fitness, and as has been mentioned earlier, no more than reasonable probability is claimed for this argument. None the less, it seems undeniable that the virginal husband of Mary and the virgin father of Jesus *ought* to have been protected from the downward pull of a deprived nature. This reasoning is so cogent that no competent Catholic theologian would admit that St. Joseph at any time felt the slightest improper tendency toward our Lady. The very idea is repugnant, and one instinctively shrinks from mentioning it. We should never forget that as far as solid logic permits, we must think of Joseph as much like Mary as possible. In a man with so superlative a relationship to Jesus and Mary even the indeliberate tendency to commit sin in *any* period of his life appears contrary to his vocation. The fault seems rather to be with us for failing to put a proper appraisal on the exalted heights to which God called St. Joseph and for which he prepared him.

Moreover, the reactions of concupiscence can lessen the fervor of the love of God even though sin itself is not committed. In this way they indirectly retard the acquisition of merit. Since Joseph's holiness and merit are to be accepted as supreme (after Mary), all concupiscence and similar elements that would retard the Saint's growth in merit are generally to be excluded. Although the restraining of concupiscence would be a most unusual gift freely bestowed by God, in granting it God would foresee the perfect manner in which Joseph would co-operate with the grace.

Regarding deliberate and semideliberate venial sin, Lepicier and those who agree with him hold that the Saint failed in no way at any time in his life. To support their opinion, they apply the above arguments for the restraining of concupiscence even more strictly with respect to venial sin. To put the fact simply, St. Joseph would seem to have been unfit for his office as virginal husband and virgin father if he had *ever* sinned *even* venially at *any* time in his life. Freedom from all sin would be required not only during the time of his mission, but equally during the time of his preparation so that he could worthily fulfill his office.

The honor of parents falls on their children (Prov. 17:6); equally so, their disgrace. Jesus belonged to Joseph as a son to his father; Jesus is the source of all holiness. How could He have chosen a father on earth who at some time or other turned away from Him even in slight infidelity? We are underestimating the dignity and intimacy of the bond between St. Joseph and our Lord, so it appears, if we suppose the existence of actual sin at *any* time in the father's life, before or during his life with his divine foster Son. Similarly, the idea of actual sin, even venial sin, seems repugnant to Joseph's close family life with Mary, before, no less than during that marriage.

Holy Scripture gives not the slightest indication that Joseph ever sinned. The body of Church writers in commenting on the Gospels have never accused Joseph of fault or imperfection in the actions narrated of him. With the evidence at least hinting that Joseph far excelled ordinary men, we ought not to prefer the ordinary law of human frailty to signs pointing to an all-sinless life in the man most Christlike.

Theologians commonly agree that the Apostles and John the Baptist were confirmed in grace. Because of the special providence of God, their wills were shielded from falling into grievous sin, and probably from falling into deliberate venial sin. All agree that St. Joseph *in some way* is included in this class at the minimum. *A fortiori,* should we refuse to grant Joseph's freedom from all actual sin, realizing that his holiness far surpasses even that of these great saints?

Cantera adds a new and original reason for holding this view.[30] There are many authors, he writes, who affirm the ligation of concupiscence in St. Joseph, not hesitating to concede this privilege to him as a necessary premise for the freedom from actual sin which they recognize in him. According to the ordinary arguments, as we have seen, it would be improper and unfitting if the one chosen to protect the virginity of Mary and the man closest to Jesus felt sinful inclinations or gave in to them. Even more, such concupiscence and sin would be a barrier to the Saint's recognized holiness after Mary. But to consider this logic more carefully, is not such a manner of thinking unworthy of Jesus and Mary no less than of Joseph? The purity of Mary was so great, her humility so deep, her modesty so pronounced, that far from provoking any sinful thought she must have inflamed hearts with the love of God. Contact, too, with Jesus would not tend to incite selfish reactions; the very opposite would be true. Hence, Cantera suggests, the ultimate reason for defending so extraordinary a prerogative as the repression of concupiscence in St. Joseph and the freedom from all mortal and venial sin lies in St. Joseph's dignity, in his ministry, in his character of husband of the Virgin and "father of God," as St. Ephrem called him centuries ago.[31]

As for the time, then, when Joseph would be given this privilege, we can make no certain decision. The more likely occasion would be when he began to use his reason. That would be when concupiscence would normally first begin to stir. If we were to delay Joseph's freedom from actual inclination to sin, and, more so, if we were to delay Joseph's freedom from all sin until the time of his marriage to our Lady, we would be forced to admit the presence of a disgraceful fact in his youth — an element that seems to make him unworthy to become husband and father of the Holy Family.[32]

THE RESURRECTION AND ASSUMPTION
OF ST. JOSEPH

Independently of any reference in Scripture, the doctrine on the resurrection of St. Joseph and the assumption of his glorified body into heaven could be proposed on grounds of

fitness. Usually, however, it has been based on the words of
St. Matthew, "Many bodies of the saints who had fallen
asleep arose; and coming forth out of the tombs after his
resurrection, they came into the holy city and appeared to
many" (27:52, 53).

The interpretation has been widely adopted that these
words do not describe what happened at the instant Christ
died and was placed in the tomb, but that they are in anticipation of what happened after Jesus rose from the dead.[33]
Scripture scholars point out that Matthew often manifests
the trait of describing at one time events that were actually
quite removed from each other when they occurred.

But for us the important question concerns the "resurrection" of these "saints." From the time of the Fathers of the
Church the predominant opinion has been that these souls
were reunited to their bodies, never to die again; and that
when Christ ascended into heaven, they entered heaven with
Him, body and soul, for all eternity. Hence, their resurrection would not be a mere return to earthly life, but a
revivifying and glorification of their bodies as will happen
on the Last Day to the rest of the just. If this interpretation
is correct, it is logical to assume (as numerous authors have
done) that St. Joseph was granted the glorification of his
body at the moment of Christ's resurrection. Of all, he
would surpassingly deserve the privilege.

Contrariwise, St. Augustine wished to understand that the
Easter resurrection of the just was merely temporary (as in
the case of Lazarus), and that these persons had to die once
again. Otherwise, he asks, how could Peter assert to the Jews
(Acts 2:29, 35) that "it was predicted not of David but of
Christ that His body would not see corruption, since David's
tomb was in their midst; and thus he did not convince them
if David's body was no longer there? Now, it seems rigorous
that David, from whose seed Christ is descended, would not
be in that rising of the just, if an eternal resurrection was
conferred on them. Also, that saying in the Epistle to the

Hebrews, 'that they should not be perfected without us' (11:40), regarding the just of the Old Testament would be hard to explain, if they were already established in that incorruption of the resurrection which is promised for the end when we shall be made perfect."[34] "Many bodies of the saints arose for a time."[35]

St. Thomas had asserted in his earlier years that these saints arose "as entering heaven with Christ."[36] He later deserted this view and thought that "Augustine's reasons seem much more cogent."[37]

Augustine's objections, however, have been met with a group of replies. Since this particular point can have so strong an influence on the doctrine of St. Joseph's assumption, it is worth our while to explain it at some length. In the first place, Augustine begins by presupposing that if the just arose at the time of our Lord's resurrection, David *must have been* in their number. There is no proof for this conjecture. Instead, the Gospel intimates that those who arose were contemporaries of the living, and were recognized as such.

Second, St. Peter's sermon to the people (Acts 2:29–35) *does not claim* that David's body is still on this earth. Peter merely refers to David's *tomb,* so that even if the body had been miraculously taken from it, no contradiction or false claim would have been involved.

Finally, multiple interpretations exist of the text Augustine invoked from the Epistle to the Hebrews, "That they should not be perfected without us." In context the phrase appears to say that the just of the Old Testament did not share in their time in the blessings of Christ, but through Him they did so later. In the Knox translation, "We were needed, to make the history of their lives complete"; or according to Lilly, "God would not have them reach perfection apart from us."[38]

Accordingly, in his work on the assumption of the Blessed Virgin, Jugie does not hesitate to adopt the interpretation opposite to that of St. Augustine. He calls it more probable and quasi-certain that the just souls mentioned by Matthew rose with Christ, to die no more.[39]

Since these saints of the Old Testament had died in the friendship of God, their souls had been supernaturally beatified ever since the moment of Christ's death, when His soul descended into limbo. Now, if on Easter they had been reunited to their bodies, only to re-enter mortal life (as Lazarus had done), they would have become pilgrims on earth once again, even though they possessed the beatific vision — they would have been mortal bodies animated by beatified souls. Suarez justly remarks that only a glorified body belongs to a beatified soul.[40] Moreover, these resurrected saints were not seen by everyone as were Lazarus and other people whom Christ brought back to life during His Public Life. Instead, they appeared only in a limited way as did Christ Himself after His own resurrection. In working this miracle God evidently wished to provide an additional proof of the resurrection of the body. It is difficult to perceive reasons for a temporary revivification; while on the other hand, the definitive resurrection of these souls would highlight the fact that ordinary humans as well as our Lord can obtain the glorification of the body.

In Jugie's analysis of the Fathers and theologians who favor this opinion, he writes, "If we had to decide this question simply by authorities, it seems that the thesis of a permanent resurrection would be brought to the fore both by the quality and the number of the commentators who have upheld it in the past and still uphold it in our own times. In our own day it has clearly prevailed."[41]

Concerning the assumption of St. Joseph into heaven, the strongest contrary view is that of Benedict XIV, speaking as a private theologian: "It cannot safely be asserted that St. Joseph ascended into heaven with body and soul."[42] Prat calls the belief "an empty conjecture," if we suppose that Joseph or any other saint was brought back to life on Easter

Day and taken with Christ into heaven forty days later.[43]

Jugie styles this as "somewhat harsh," adding, "We do not think that Suarez, Francis de Sales, and Cardinal Lepicier made 'an empty conjecture' in conjecturing that St. Joseph was among those brought back to life."[44] An impressive number of modern authors present Joseph's assumption as at least probable, even as a "sufficiently authoritative tradition."[45] Holzmeister, however, thinks that if commentators on Matthew 27:52 make no mention of St. Joseph, their silence indicates their disapproval of the doctrine of the Saint's assumption.[46]

This reasoning seems extreme. Only an explicit statement that the Saint's assumption is probable or improbable should be accepted. Silence on the point can easily mean that the mention of St. Joseph did not fall within the projected scope of a theological or scriptural study and was therefore omitted. The positive arguments for Joseph's assumption appear in John Gerson, Bernardine of Siena, Suarez, and Francis de Sales.

Gerson proposed the belief in his sermon at Constance in 1416. "We read that when Christ died, many bodies of the saints arose, entered the holy city Jerusalem, and appeared to many. Perhaps it is with reference to this that the Apostle says, 'Women had their dead restored to them by resurrection' (Hebr. 11:35). Let pious belief ponder, I beg of you, whether we should not assume that Joseph was one of these, that he appeared to his dearest spouse Mary and consoled her, and that finally he ascended with Christ into heaven — doubtless in soul, and I know not but God knows if in body also — and that he receives his place at the right hand of Jesus Himself, that is, in greatest beatitude."[47]

Bernardine of Siena gives a long portrayal of Joseph's assumption. "It may be accepted in pious faith, not however affirmed as certain, that the perfect divine son Jesus distinguished His foster father with the same privilege as His most holy mother; that just as He assumed her gloriously into

heaven with body and soul, so on the day of Resurrection
He likewise took most holy Joseph with Himself in the glory
of the Resurrection. Thus, just as this holy family — Christ,
the Virgin, and Joseph — lived together in laborious life and
affectionate grace on earth, so do they now rule in affectionate glory in heaven with body and soul.

"According to the norm of the Apostle, 'As you are par-
takers of the sufferings, so will you also be of the consolation'
(2 Cor. 1:7). For it is written in Matthew 27: 'Many bodies
of the saints arose, who had fallen asleep,' that is, were dead.
According to Jerome[48] this happened when the Lord arose,
because the Lord was the 'firstborn of the dead and the ruler
of the kings of the earth,' as is said in the Apocalypse (1:5).
This nevertheless is narrated by anticipation, to show that
this event took place by the power and merit of His Passion.
These souls arose with Christ, I say, as witnesses of His Resurrection. Matthew plainly adds this when he says, 'And
coming forth out of the tombs after His Resurrection, they
came into the holy city and appeared to many.' We may
piously believe that among these risen ones was this most
holy man [Joseph]. . . . If then for a reasonable cause and
by a special privilege, the resurrection of both body and
soul was hastened for Joseph and some others, there is no
disturbance of order; nay more, it is according to reason. For
it is proper that ordinary events be kept in their order in
such a way that they can still give place to the privilege of
the great king."[49]

Suarez presents the assumption of St. Joseph as solidly
probable. "I will not neglect to call attention to the rather
general belief that it is probable that this saint gloriously
reigns with Christ in soul and body. Since he died before
Christ, it is very likely that he was one of those who arose
at the time of the death or resurrection of Christ and who,
as many believe, passed on to the immortal life of the soul
and body."[50]

No one has ever proposed the doctrine more vigorously

than Francis de Sales, Saint and Doctor of the Church. "What more remains to be said," he asks, "except that we can never for a moment doubt that this glorious saint has great influence in heaven with Him who raised him there in body and soul — a fact which is the more probable because we have no relic of that body left us here below? Indeed, it seems to me that no one can doubt this as a truth, for how could He who had been so obedient to St. Joseph all through His life refuse him this grace?

"Doubtless, when our Lord descended into limbo, He was addressed by St. Joseph in this fashion: 'Lord, remember, please, that when You came down from heaven to earth, I received You into my house and into my family, and that at the moment of Your birth I received You into my arms. Now that You are returning to heaven, take me there with You. I received You into my family; receive me now into Yours. I carried You in my arms; take me into Yours. And as I carefully nourished and protected You in Your mortal life, take care of me and lead me into life immortal.'

"And if it is true, as we are bound to believe, that in virtue of the Blessed Sacrament which we receive, our bodies will come to life again on the day of judgment, how can we doubt that our Lord did as much for him, making St. Joseph rise into heaven in body and soul? For he had the honor and the grace of carrying Him so often in his blessed arms, those arms in which our Lord took so much pleasure. Oh, how many tender kisses His sacred lips bestowed on him, to reward him for his toils and labors! Yes, St. Joseph is in heaven in body and soul; there is no doubt."[51]

To summarize this view, the doctrine of the resurrection and assumption of St. Joseph into heaven in body and soul is put forward as theologically probable, and is based on grounds of fitness. Good reason exists for holding that according to the text from Matthew's Gospel (27:52) certain souls were united to their bodies when Christ rose from the dead, and that they were later taken into heaven when Jesus ascended there. Joseph's intimacy with the sacred body of our Lord, as well as his spiritual likeness to Mary afford special reason to think he was granted this privilege. It is true that theology does not have at its disposal any means of deciding on the ultimate certainty of St. Joseph's assumption. It would appear that if anyone in addition to our Blessed Lady has ever been taken up into heaven in body and soul, that person would be her virginal husband, St. Joseph.

REFERENCES — CHAPTER FOUR

1. Gotti, *De Veritate Religionis Christianae*, Rome, 1736, tom. 4, p. 1, c. 4, No. 7, p. 113, quoted by Llamera in *EJ*, 2 (1948), 175.

2. Cantera, 373.

3. José Domingo María Corbató, *El Inmaculado S. José*, Valencia, 1907; condemnation in *ASS*, 41, 43; February 26, 1907. Corbató suggested that the Holy Spirit gave St. Joseph a physical supernatural fatherhood by transplanting seed from St. Joseph into Mary's body; Cantera, 379, gives a list of authors who have criticized Corbató and have called the book erroneous, contrary to Scripture and Christian tradition, fantastic, and extravagant.

4. So mentioned though not clearly affirmed by Bernardine of Busti, in *Mariale*, P. 4, Sermo 12 (*SI* 953); also mentioned without being defended by John of Carthagena, *Homil. Cathol.*, tom. 1, 4, "De S. Joseph," hom. 12, n. 2 (*SI* 781).

5. Session 5, Canon 2 (*DB* 792).

6. *DB* 1641.

7. Cf. Raff. Petrone, C.M., in *Divus Thomas* (Piacenza), ser. 3, 5 (January, 1928). These statements were made in an article on the fatherhood of St. Joseph which was condemned by the Supreme Congregation of the Holy Office and was subsequently retracted by the author for any error or offense it contained against Catholic sense (*ibid.*, 361). Precisely what was the error was not stated. But it is to be noted that the distinction between the *exclusiveness* and the *merely special nature* of the definition of the Immaculate Conception may legitimately be made. Cf. Llamera, *EJ* 2 (1948), 178; Merkelbach, *Mariologia*, Strasburg, 1946, P. 2, p. 109: "It is not perfectly clear that the Church wished to define [the Immaculate Conception] as unique and completely exclusive."

8. Lépicier, *Tractatus de S. Joseph*, P. 2, art. 1, 2; 141.

9. Cantera, 381, 377; cites De Lugo, *De Ver. Fidei Divinae*, Disp. 20, sect. 3, for the rashness of holding the immaculate conception of St. Joseph.

10. Gerson, Sermon of September 8, 1416, Consid. 2 (*SI* 154); Llamera in *EJ*, 2 (1948), 179, lists some of those who hold the affirmative view: Isidor de Isolani, *Summa de donis S. Josephi*, P. 1, c. 9; Bernardine of Busti, *Mariale*, P. 4, Sermo 12 (*SI* 954); Alphonsus de Liguori, *Sermo 1 de S. Josepho*, Pt. 2 (in *The Glories of Mary*, ed. Grimm (New York: Benziger, 1887), 2, 350; John of Carthagena, *Hom. cathol.*, lib. 18, hom. ult. (*SI* 781); Petrus Morales, S.J.,

In Caput 1 Matth. (Paris: Vivès, 1869), 1, 214; Giacomo Sinibaldi, *La Grandezza di San Giuseppe,* Rome, 1927, 172; Démaret, 86; also Janssens, Pore, Tesnière, Sauvé.

The negative opinion: This can be said to be implicitly taught in St. Thomas, but he does not explicitly teach that Joseph was not sanctified in the womb. Cf. *ST,* 3, q. 27, a. 6, resp.; Cajetan, *In III,* q. 27, a. 6; Benedict XIV, *De Beatif. Serv. Dei,* 4, 2, c. 20, n. 31; Gotti, *De Ver. Relig. Christ.,* 4, P. 1, c. 4, No. 7; Lépicier, *Tractatus,* P. 2, a. 1, No. 7, p. 144.

11. Suarez, Disp. 8, sect. 2, No. 6, 8.

12. John of Carthagena, Lib. 18, *"De Cultu et Devot. erga B. V. et D. Joseph,"* hom. ult. *(SI* 366).

13. Isidore de Isolani, P. 1, c. 9.

14. Aquinas, *ST,* 3, q. 27, art. 6.

15. Lépicier, *Tractatus,* 146.

16. Cantera, 386.

17. On the other hand, C. Lattey, S.J., in *A Catholic Commentary on Holy Scripture,* ed. Orchard, 575 (par. 454c), takes the view in favor of such sanctification of Jeremias — "the more likely view" — although he admits that "There is no strictly systematic theology in the OT." Against the view, cf. *L'Ami du Clergé,* 38 (1921), 106, whose author, evidently A. Michel, believes that "sanctify" means merely "destine." In the article reprinted practically verbatim from this issue of *L'Ami,* Michel holds against prenatal sanctification *(DTC,* 8, 1517).

18. Benedict XIV, 4, 2, c. 20, n. 31.

19. Aquinas, *ST,* 3, q. 27, art. resp.

20. Demaret, 86.

21. Cornelius a Lapide, *In Matth.* 1:16 *(Commentaria in Scripturam Sacram* [Paris: Vivès, 1862], 15, 58).

22. Based partially on Cantera, 388–395; Llamera, 2 (1948), 165–172; 184–185; Michel, *DTC,* 8, 1518; Démaret, 89 ff.

23. Richard, art. "Impeccabilité," in *DTC,* 7, 1274.

24. Canon J. M. Hervé, *Man. Theol. Dog.,* ed. 17, Paris, 1935, 2, 652.

25. Session 6, canon 23 *(DB* 833).

26. Michel, *DTC,* 8, 1518.

27. Session 5 *(DB* 792).

28. Cf. Zubizarreta, *Theologia dogmatica scholastica,* Bilbao, 1937, 2, 506.

29. Llamera, *EJ,* 2 (1948), 185.

30. Cantera, 391.

31. Quoted in *JJ,* 29; from F. J. Foakes Jackson and Kirsopp Lake, *The Beginnings of Christianity* (London: Macmillan, 1926), 3, 387.

32. Cantera, 390–392; Llamera, *ES,* 2 (1948), 185; Sinibaldi, 174; Lépicier, *Tractatus,* III, 2; p. 152 ff.

33. A. Jones in *A Catholic Commentary on Holy Scripture,* 903 (par. 722 f.); Aquinas, *Comment. in Matth.* 27:52.

34. Augustine, *Ep. ad Evod.,* 9 (Ep. 164, ML 33, 712).

35. Augustine, *In Joann.,* 124, 2 (ML 35, 1970).

36. Aquinas, *Catena Aurea, Comment. in Matth.* 27:52; *In IV. Sent.,* dist. 43, q. 1, a. 3, q. 4, ad 3; *ST,* Suppl., q. 77, a. 1, ad 3.

37. Aquinas, *ST,* 3, q. 53, art. 3, ad 2.

38. Martin Jugie, A.A., *La mort et l'assomption de la sainte vierge,* Vatican City, 1944, 51 ff. The Lilly translation of the Epistles is contained in Kleist-Lilly, *The New Testament* (Milwaukee: Bruce, 1954).

39. Jugie, ix.

40. Suarez, *In III*, q. 53, a. 3, n. 15.

41. Jugie, 52.

42. Benedict XIV, 4, 2, c. 20, n. 33.

43. F. Prat, S.J., *Jesus Christ*, tr. by John H. Heenan, S.J. (Milwaukee: Bruce, 1950), 2, 399.

44. Jugie, 54.

45. Sinibaldi, 206, quoted by Urban Holzmeister, S.J., *De Sancto Ioseph Quaestiones Biblicae*, Rome, 1945, 116, citing twelve authors.

46. Holzmeister, 116.

47. Gerson, Sermon of September 8, 1416, Consid. 3 (*SI* 184).

48. Jerome, *In Matth.* 4 (*ML* 26, 222).

49. Bernardine of Siena, *Sermo de S. Joseph*, c. 3, art. 3 (*SI* 59–61; 65).

50. Suarez, disp. 8, sect. 2, n. 8.

51. Francis de Sales, *The Spiritual Conferences*, 19, 383.

CHAPTER FIVE

St. Joseph's Patronage

LIKE every patron saint, Joseph receives from God a quasi-right to protect his clients.[1] This precise relationship of patron saint to client is difficult to express in our language, but the fact is certain. The patron is like a father toward his charge, and a strong note of fatherly love characterizes his watchful care. Etymologically, the word "patron" means he who has the place of father and who frees us from danger, defends our rights, and helps us in our needs. Only Jesus Christ is our primary mediator or "patron" with God. However, far from suffering damage to the unique headship He possesses, Jesus is all the more glorified and exalted by the invocation of the saints as patrons and as secondary mediators.

The communion of saints is the bond that unites the Church Triumphant with the Church Militant and the Church Suffering. Because of this bond God grants the saints in heaven a special intercessory power so that they can further by their prayers the spiritual and temporal interests of their brethren on earth. They invoke the merits they gained during their time of pilgrimage, and by an act of supplication they present to God their requests for their clients. In this interest and help we rightly discern a manifestation of the all-embracing love which Christ desires to flourish in His Church.

Individual saints can freely be chosen as patrons by anyone. In the case of some, however, it is fitting that they specially watch over particular groups of people or types of enterprises. Ordinarily, this fitness exists because of a circumstance of the saints' lives or some providential direction of their energies and prayers. Thus, the patrons' interests are more specifically those of their clients.

PAPAL PRONOUNCEMENTS

In the case of St. Joseph his patronage is the logical extension of his duties on earth. Although he was officially declared Patron of the Universal Church by Pius IX in 1870, Pius did not actually create him as such. The Pope proclaimed what had already been a reality. St. Joseph's office as Patron of the Universal Church as well as the dignity belonging to this title was a corollary of the office and the dignity which God bestowed on him in making Joseph the head of the Holy Family.

The decree of Pius IX makes this clear. "Because of this sublime dignity which God conferred on His most faithful servant, the Church has always most highly honored and praised Blessed Joseph next to his spouse, the Virgin Mother of God, and has besought his intercession in times of trouble. ... Pius IX, Pope, has therefore declared St. Joseph Patron of the Universal Church." The same terminology of "declaring" the Saint's patronage occurs in the Pope's decree of 1871.[2]

Even more detailed is Leo XIII's encyclical on St. Joseph. We read in it, "There are special reasons why Blessed Joseph should be explicitly named the Patron of the Church, and why the Church in turn should expect much from his patronage and guardianship. For he indeed was the husband of Mary, and the father, as was supposed, of Jesus Christ. From this arise all his dignity, grace, holiness, and glory. ...

"The divine household which Joseph governed as with paternal authority contained the beginnings of the new Church. The Virgin most holy is the mother of all Christians, since she is the mother of Jesus and since she gave birth to them on the mount of Calvary amid the indescribable sufferings of the Redeemer. Jesus is, as it were, the firstborn of Christians, who are his brothers by adoption and redemption.

"From these considerations we conclude that the Blessed Patriarch must regard all the multitude of Christians who constitute the Church as confided to his care in a certain special manner. This is his numberless family scattered throughout all lands, over which he rules with a sort of paternal authority, because he is the husband of Mary and the father of Jesus Christ. Thus, it is conformable to reason and in every way becoming to Blessed Joseph that as once it was his sacred trust to guard with watchful care the family of Nazareth, no matter what befell, so now by virtue of his heavenly patronage he is in turn to protect and to defend the Church of Christ."[3]

THE HISTORY OF ST. JOSEPH'S
PATRONAGE

This concept of St. Joseph's relationship to the Church lay hidden and unnoticed for centuries. Certainly among the first men to call attention to it were John Gerson and St. Bernardine of Siena. However, in view of recent data concerning St. Bernardine's literary sources — Ubertino of Casale and to some extent, Bartholomew of Pisa — it would seem that we can push back the first mention of Joseph's patronage into the latter half of the fourteenth century. This mention is found in a book by Bartholomew of Pisa († 1401) in the following words: "Our mother the Church is in every way in debt toward Blessed Mary, from whom she received Christ; immediately next, she is in debt to Joseph."[4] This idea appears in the sermon of Bernardine, the brother Franciscan who flourished some fifty years after Bartholomew: "If the entire Church is in debt to the Virgin Mother, since it is by means of Mary that she has been rendered worthy to receive the Savior, likewise, after her she owes gratitude and singular reverence to this man [Joseph]."[5]

However, the formal proposal of St. Joseph's guardianship

of the Church was made in Gerson's sermon at the Council of Constance in 1416. The sermon had as its purpose the adoption of a feast of the espousal of Joseph and Mary. With deep anxiety the chancellor noted the disastrous results of the great Western Schism of 1378, a wound to the Church which was still unhealed. Gerson asked the approval of the feast of the espousal "in order that through the merits of Mary and through the intercession of so great, so powerful, and in a certain way so omnipotent an intercessor with his bride . . . the Church might be led to her only true and safe Lord, the supreme pastor, her spouse in place of Christ."[6] The suggestion made by Gerson was not acted on, but once it had been put forth, the idea continued to recur to others. What really began to receive marked emphasis was Joseph's part as guardian of the Holy Family. This contained in germ the concept of Joseph's further guardianship of Christ's Church.

It was next elaborated in the *Summa of the Gifts of St. Joseph,* a short theological work in Latin written by the Dominican Isidore de Isolani in 1522. When depicting the exceptional honors he felt sure would be granted the saint, Isidore heralded the future with this prophecy: "For the honor of His name God has chosen St. Joseph as head and special patron of the Church Militant."[7]

The theme of Joseph's guidance of the Holy Family and the Church continued to run through the devotion as it flourished up to the middle of the eighteenth century. Here, in common with the temporal fortunes of the Church, it suffered a relapse; but with the reign of Pius IX, a hundred years later, it again surged forward. During the 1860's, various petitions from bishops, priests, and the faithful were sent to the Holy See, asking for St. Joseph's full glorification in the liturgy and for the declaration of his Patronage of the Universal Church. Three special petitions were presented to the Vatican Council in 1869–1870. It seems that these three were the petitions which immediately led Pius IX to make his declaration on the Feast of the Immaculate Conception in 1870.[8]

ST. JOSEPH AS PATRIARCH

Closely related to Joseph's title as Patron of the Universal Church is his title of Patriarch. Ordinarily, the name "patriarch" is reserved for a man who is the father of numerous descendants. The patriarchs of the Old Testament deserve the title not only because of their venerable fatherhood, but also (in a spiritual manner) because of the Messias who was to be born of their line. They were literally "patriarchs in preparation" in view of God's promise of the Saviour who was to spring from the Jewish people.

St. Joseph was a patriarch in the full sense, understanding the term in this spiritual meaning. Our Lord took human nature of the virginal wife of Joseph, and in this way the Saint exercised the rights of father over Him whose spiritual posterity would embrace all the elect.

Leo XIII explains in his encyclical how Joseph's position as patriarch is linked with his office as patron. "Conformably with the Church's sacred liturgy, the opinion has been held by not a few Fathers of the Church that the ancient Joseph, son of the Patriarch Jacob, foreshadowed both in person and in office our own St. Joseph. By his glory he was a prototype of the grandeur of the future guardian of the Holy Family. In addition to the circumstance that both men bore the same name — a name by no means devoid of significance — it is well known to you that they resembled each other very closely in other ways as well. Notable in this regard are the facts that the earlier Joseph received special favor and benevolence from his lord, and that, when placed by him as ruler over his household, fortune and prosperity abundantly accrued to the master's house because of Joseph.

"There was even a more evident similarity when by the king's order he was given supreme power over the entire kingdom. When calamity brought on a deficient harvest and a scarcity of grain, he exercised such excellent foresight in behalf of the Egyptians and their neighbors that the king decreed he should be styled 'savior of the world.' Thus in that ancient patriarch we may recognize the distinct image of St. Joseph. As the one was prosperous and successful in the domestic concerns of his lord and in an exceptional manner was set over the whole kindgom, so the other, destined to guard the name of Christ, could well be chosen to defend and to protect the Church, which is truly the house of God and the kingdom of God on earth."[9]

In the early 1700's, the Holy See was considering the reinsertion of the saint's name into the Litany of the Saints, from which it had been dropped at some earlier date. In the study of this question Cardinal Lambertini (the future Benedict XIV) published a strong defense of Joseph's position as patriarch. He wrote, "That St. Joseph can be called patriarch is proved from the fact that the patriarchs, according to the Holy Fathers and both ancient and more recent writers, were those who were the progenitors of the families of the Chosen People. Since, therefore, St. Joseph was the putative father of Christ our Lord, who is the head of the predestined and of the elect, the name of patriarch is for this reason rightly and deservedly attributed to St. Joseph, and by this very name is he addressed by most writers.

"St. Joseph was not the natural father of Christ our Lord and did not generate Him, but this can prove only that he was not the father of the faithful by natural generation, as were the other patriarchs. It does not hinder him from being patriarch in a more perfect and more exalted manner according to the explanation we have already given."[10]

In our own day this title has been more or less superseded by direct references to the Saint as husband of Mary and foster father or virgin father of Jesus. Probably the main reason for this evolution in popular usage is that the older word brings to mind the picture of a man who is very advanced in years. Catholics long since have rightly rejected the legendary picture of St. Joseph as an old, old man because such a picture does not agree with his vocation and its requirements as explained in the gospels. Another possible reason is the implicit linkage with the Old Testament which is contained in the title of patriarch. More and more, St. Joseph's closeness to Christ has been recognized; and in the same proportion he tends to recede from the Old Testament setting given him in earlier years.

THE DIGNITY AND EFFICACY OF THE PATRONAGE

Joseph's patronage, as we mentioned in an earlier chapter, is one of the indications of the Saint's exalted dignity, for his titles both as patriarch and as Patron of the Universal Church recognize in him an excellence that is absent in other men. The wider the extent of the patronage, so much the greater is its dignity; and since Joseph's patronage is concerned with the entire Church, as patron he is reverenced to a degree subordinate only to the honor given Mary. The patronage also is a measure of the Saint's dignity on the score of the perfection on which it is based. Joseph's role is not based merely on a certain fittingness, as is the case with other patron saints. Instead, his God-given position as husband of Mary and father in Jesus' family directly places the interests of Christ's Church close to his heart.

But what of efficacy? The power of Joseph's intercession appears from his holiness as well as from his position on earth and his glory in heaven. The higher a soul exists in glory, by so much is that soul acceptable to God. Joseph's holiness and glory, as second only to Mary's, would point to equally powerful intercession with God for Joseph's clients. As for Joseph's office on earth, he alone of all men exercised paternal authority over Christ; and he alone shared family life with the blessed Mediatrix of all graces as her virginal husband. This relationship on earth, continued in a certain way in heaven, gives St. Joseph a tremendous intercessory power which the Church has officially recognized. One of the most indicative actions has been the approval and indulgencing of a *Memorare* in imitation of the same type of prayer exclusively addressed to our Lady: "Remember, O most pure spouse of the Virgin Mary, St. Joseph, my beloved patron, that never has it been heard that anyone invoked thy patronage and sought thy aid without being comforted. Inspired by this confidence, I come to thee and fervently commend myself to thee. O despise not my petition, dear foster father of our Redeemer, but accept it graciously. Amen."[11]

THE UNIVERSALITY OF THE PATRONAGE

It would appear that St. Joseph's patronage as understood in its full extent embraces all those who owe their salvation to the redemptive work of Jesus and to the intercession of the Blessed Virgin. The reason is clear. Joseph was chosen to be virgin father and virginal husband in order that the redemptive work of our Lord in co-operation with Mary might be accomplished. Hence, the saint's guardianship (which is the outgrowth of his protection of Jesus and our Lady) logically embraces all who participate in the fruits of the Redemption.

Meditative consideration of the full meaning of Joseph's title reveals still further consequences in another direction. Since the saint is patron of the whole Church, his interests must be more universal than those of other saints. Other patrons concern themselves with one group of persons; Joseph is patron of all. Hence, writers have amplified his title so that they describe him as *universal* patron *because* Patron of the Universal Church. In this respect it is fortunate that from the very first petitions sent to the Holy See in the past century, the requests from the bishops, priests, and lay people used the words "Universal Church" instead of "Catholic Church." True as it is that "catholic" and "universal" mean the same, "catholic" has taken on a popular connotation more as a proper adjective designating the Church but not implying its universality. More exactly, perhaps we should say that the popular mind does not advert to the "universal" meaning of "catholic." At any rate, the choice of language was a happy one, and the Church documents have retained the wording of the original petitions which emphasize St. Joseph as the patron *of* all and *for* all.

Because Joseph was a member of an impoverished family of kings, the story of his life heartens all who suffer financial reverses. Earning his livelihood and supporting his holy charges at the carpenter's bench, he fittingly inspires all who work for a living. In his actions we can discover a guiding principle that can hold true for every employer. He can look to Joseph, who while superior in authority, recognized that he was inferior in dignity and used his authority with the utmost moderation and prudence. Thus, while on the one hand St. Joseph inspires employers to give just wages and to provide healthful working conditions, on the other hand his example reminds employees to return fair and industrious services for wages received, all in an atmosphere of charity and harmony and common working together for the common good.

Against the purveyors of the false ideologies of our day, Joseph stands out as the antithesis of racial prejudice and international hatred. Himself a Jew, he suffered because of the political dreams of Herod, a monarch mad for power at any cost. Welcoming the foreign Magi and then living in exile in a not too friendly land, he witnessed the distress caused by prejudice against color and against race.

Joseph's place as father in the Holy Family shows all fathers how steadfastly they must strive to imitate him in cherishing and educating their children. No husband can ever offer his wife a degree of fidelity and self-sacrifice greater than that which Joseph offered our Lady. Hence, in him we behold the worthy patron of the Christian family. The close union of souls between the father and mother in the Holy Family is the goal which every Christian husband and wife should look to. If they attain success in imitating such love, they will find that their true love shows itself in *every* aspect of their life together.

As head of Nazareth, the first Christian religious community, St. Joseph exemplifies the ideal religious superior, the servant of the servants of God. Simultaneously his absolute and unquestioning obedience to the messengers of God marks him out as the model for priests and for religious. When the end comes to the period of service, Joseph by his death in the presence of Jesus and Mary is made the grand protector in the hour of death for other men — the friend who leads departing souls peacefully to their Judge.

In our own age St. Joseph's patronage of labor has been particularly emphasized together with Joseph's patronage of the family. Closely coupled with the former emphasis was the honor granted to him in 1937 by Pius XI. At that time the Pope declared him the patron of the Church's campaign against atheistic communism, for "he belongs to the working-class, and he bore the burdens of poverty for himself and the Holy Family, whose tender and vigilant head he was."[12] The great contribution of Pius XII was made on May 1, 1955, when he announced his intention of instituting the new feast of St. Joseph the Worker in order to christianize secularistic May Day attitudes toward management and labor.

We possess sound Church authority for claiming St. Joseph as the universal patron in the Church. Leo XIII's encyclical, after tracing the Saint's present position to his earlier vocation on earth, continues, "This is the reason why the faithful of all places and conditions commend and confide themselves to the guardianship of Blessed Joseph. In Joseph fathers of families have an eminent model of paternal care and providence. Married couples find in him the perfect image of love, harmony, and conjugal loyalty. Virgins can look to him for their pattern and as the guardian of virginal integrity. With the picture of Joseph set before them, those of noble lineage can learn to preserve their dignity even under adverse circumstances. Let the wealthy understand what goods they should chiefly seek and earnestly amass, while with no less special right the needy, the laborers, and all possessed of merely modest means should fly to his protection and learn to imitate him."[13] The same pope's letter on the Holy Family is entirely devoted to the subject of family life, placing Joseph with Mary and Jesus as a family exemplar.[14]

In the words of Benedict XV, "Since Joseph, whose death took place in the presence of Jesus and Mary, is justly regarded as the most efficacious protector of the dying, it is our purpose here to lay a special injunction on Our Venerable Brethren that they assist in every possible manner those pious associations which have been instituted to obtain the intercession of St. Joseph for the dying."[15]

ST. JOSEPH AND ST. MICHAEL

It is logical to wonder how the patronage of St. Joseph differs, if at all, from the patronage of St. Michael the Archangel over the Church. Following Bialas, we would agree that both saints are Patrons of the Universal Church, but St. Joseph "has been the only one to receive *solemn* declaration."

Moreover, "as an *angelic spirit,* the Archangel Michael excels St. Joseph, who is *human* by nature. St. Michael excels in that he can help his clients by his natural powers of 'movement.' In the *supernatural order,* however, and especially in his power of intercession, considering his dignity, St. Joseph could excel St. Michael." The reasons for believing that Joseph does excel have been already stated. But how do the patronages of St. Joseph and St. Michael differ?

The differentiating element seems to be that Michael obtains his results more as a warrior for the Church; St. Joseph accomplishes his, as a father. "Joseph fights evil but in a rather positive way, i.e., by promoting the good . . . the

Archangel is more of the Champion and Warrior type; he resists evil by getting at the evil — he openly resists to conquer the enemy, as he did against Lucifer and his devils; he is aggressive; he does things by leadership — by leading forces against the enemy before the latter even attacks . . . he fortifies, defends, and guards."[16]

THE LITANY OF ST. JOSEPH

The shortest official summary of the Saint's patronage is found in the Litany of St. Joseph, approved by Pius X in 1909. This Litany condenses, as it were, Leo XIII's earlier catalogue of Joseph's clients — "all the faithful of all places and conditions."

The action of Pius X in sanctioning the Litany of St. Joseph for use in public services gave Joseph one of his most exclusive honors. Only four other litanies have been granted this rare and signal approval — the Litanies of the Sacred Heart and of the Holy Name of Jesus, the Blessed Virgin's Litany of Loreto, and the Litany of the Saints (with its adaptations for Holy Saturday and for the commendation of a departing soul).

The use of a litany as a form of prayer dates from the very earliest days of the Church itself. The word comes from the Greek term *lissomai*, "I pray." The first Christians probably modeled their litanies on Psalm 135, "Praise the Lord, for He is good; for His mercy endures forever." Here, after each statement of the Psalmist, the phrase is repeated, "for His mercy endures forever." This repetition of the same prayer has passed over into our modern litanies. When addressing God, we beg, "Have mercy on us"; when petitioning the saints' intercession, we say, "Pray for us." In this manner God or our Lady or St. Joseph can be honored under different titles but always with the same petition.

We can well understand the reason for the Church's strictness in limiting the number of litanies for public use. In 1600 there were more than eighty varieties in circulation.

Some of these were conducive to pompous, stilted formalism rather than genuine piety. Only the age-old Litany of the Saints and our Lady's Litany of Loreto were permitted to remain. During the past century the Litanies of the Holy Name and of the Sacred Heart of Jesus were added.

This brief consideration of the history of litanies in the Church is necessary to appreciate how unusual is the honor given St. Joseph. In the decree of St. Pius sanctioning the Litany of St. Joseph, the Holy Father mentioned his special devotion to St. Joseph, whose name he received at baptism. Then he stated his willingness to accede to the petition signed by many bishops and heads of Religious Orders. He wished to follow the course begun by his predecessors, Pius IX and Leo XIII. The Holy Father's special reason, so his decree stated, lay in his desire to urge the faithful to imitate more closely the virtues of St. Joseph. Therefore, St. Pius approved and indulgenced the new litany.[17]

There is a very interesting feature about the Litany of St. Joseph. Unlike the older litanies which grew up out of separate and more or less unrelated invocations, the Litany of St. Joseph is divided into rigidly logical groups:

I. Seven titles depict the role Joseph played on earth:

  a) Two concern his royal ancestry in preparation for the Messias:
    "Illustrious descendant of David";
    "Light of patriarchs";

  b) Two, his relationship to Mary:
    "Spouse of the Mother of God";
    "Chaste guardian of the Virgin";

  c) Two, his relationship to Jesus:
    "Foster father of the Son of God";
    "Watchful defender of Christ";

  d) and finally one title as:
    "Head of the Holy Family."

II. In the second group of invocations, six list Joseph's special virtues: justice, chastity, prudence, valiance, obedience, and faith.

III. The final group consists of eleven titles.

a) Four address him as exemplar:

"Mirror of patience";
"Lover of poverty";
"Model of workmen";
"Ornament of domestic life";

b) and seven invoke him as a protecting patron:

"Guardian of virgins";
"Safeguard of families";
"Consolation of the poor";
"Hope of the sick";
"Patron of the dying";
"Terror of demons";
"Protector of Holy Church."

But for the final word on the patronage of St. Joseph, probably no tribute to the Saint's widespread and powerful help and friendship will ever surpass the words of St. Teresa of Avila, long become classic: "It seems that to other saints our Lord has given power to help us in only one kind of necessity; but this glorious saint, I know by my own experience, assists us in all kinds of necessities. . . . I only request, for the love of God, that whoever will not believe me will test the truth of what I say, for he will see by experience how great a blessing it is to recommend oneself to this glorious Patriarch and to be devout to him. . . . Whoever wants a master to instruct him how to pray, let him choose this glorious saint for his guide, and he will not lose his way."[18]

REFERENCES — CHAPTER FIVE

1. The material of this chapter is discussed in Macabiau, 142, 236; Lepicier, 265 ff.; Mueller, 205 ff.; Bover, 48 ff.; Cantera, 417 ff.

2. Pius IX, *Quemadmodum Deus*, *ASS*, 6, 193; tr. in *MNC*, 163; the subsequent decree was *Inclytum Patriarcham*, *ASS*, 6, 324.

3. *MNC*, 172.

4. Quoted from Bartholomew de Pisa, *De vita Beatae Mariae Virginis*, Venice, 1956, lib. 2, fruct. 18, 265, in *CJ*, 2 (1953), 193.

5. Bernardine of Siena, *Sermo de S. Joseph*, art. 2 (*SI* 49).

6. John Gerson, Sermon of September 8, 1416, Concl. (*SI* 213).

7. Isidore de Isolani, *Summa de donis S. Joseph*, III, 8.

8. Cf. *MNC*, c. 9, 10, and epilogue for historical details (155–192); also *infra*, c. 6, p. 96 ff.

9. *MNC*, 173.

10. Benedict XIV, *De Beatif. Serv. Dei*, 4, 2, c. 20, n. 57 (*SI* 2881).

11. Indulg. 500 days, S. P. Ap., Jan. 20, 1933; *Enchirid. Indulg.* (1950), n. 472.

12. Pius XI, *Divini Redemptoris*, *AAS*, 29, 106; *MNC*, 184.

13. *QP*, in *MNC*, 173.

14. Leo XIII, *Neminem Fugit*, Decr. 3777, C.S.R.

15. Benedict XV, *Bonum Sane*, *AAS* 12, 313; tr. in *MNC*, 183.

16. Andrew A. Bialas, C.S.V., *The Patronage of Saint Michael the Archangel*, Clerics of St. Viator, Chicago, 1954, 132–133.

17. *AAS* 1, 290.

18. Teresa of Avila, *Autobiography*, c. 6, n. 11; *MNC*, 193.

CHAPTER SIX

The Petitions for St. Joseph's Advance in the Liturgy

EVER since 1815, various petitions from thousands of bishops, priests, and laymen have been sent to the Holy See, requesting increased honors for St. Joseph in the liturgy. A major request in these petitions has concerned the invocation of the Saint in the Mass, particularly in the following prayers:

1. The Confession (*Confiteor*);
2. The "Receive, O Holy Trinity" (*Suscipe, Sancta Trinitas*);
3. Within the Canon, the "Sharing and Venerating the Memory" (*Communicantes*);
4. And after the Canon, the "Deliver us, we beseech Thee" (*Libera nos, quaesumus*).

As is evident, the discussion is restricted to the Latin Rite liturgy. The precise request has been that St. Joseph be invoked after our Blessed Lady in each of these prayers.

As suggested by Aloysius Marchesi, a Consultor of the Congregation of Sacred Rites in 1870, the prayers would read as follows:[1]

"I confess to almighty God, to Blessed Mary ever virgin, to St. Joseph her spouse, to Blessed Michael the archangel. . . . Therefore I beseech Blessed Mary ever virgin, St. Joseph her spouse, Blessed Michael the archangel . . . to pray to the Lord our God for me."

"Receive, O holy Trinity, this offering we make to Thee
in remembrance of the Passion, Resurrection, and Ascension
of our Lord Jesus Christ, and in honor of Blessed Mary ever
virgin, of her Blessed spouse Joseph, of Blessed John the
Baptist, of the holy apostles Peter and Paul, of these and
of all the saints. . . ."

"Sharing and venerating the memory first of the glorious
Mary ever virgin, mother of our God and Lord Jesus Christ,
together with her spouse Blessed Joseph; likewise of Thy
Blessed apostles and martyrs. . . ."

"Deliver us, we beseech Thee, O Lord, from all evils, past,
present, and to come; and by the intercession of the Blessed
and glorious Mary ever virgin, Mother of God, together with
Blessed Joseph her spouse, and with Thy Blessed apostles
Peter and Paul and Andrew and all the Saints. . . ."

The best known of all the petitions were circulated by
Father Cyprian Macabiau, S.J., from 1887 to 1908, although
we are in doubt when or even whether he might have submitted them formally to the Holy See. Much confusion has
arisen over the identity of this promoter because of his
pseudonym of "C.M." and "C. Mariani." Actually, he was a
professor of theology and a writer (1846–1915), a "man of
one book and one task" — to promote the devotion to St.
Joseph, and particularly to obtain for St. Joseph the honors
of a cultus of *protodulia*. The author usually signed only his
initials; but he evidently hoped that his work would have
more authority if he adopted the pseudonym of C. Mariani
and — so it would seem — if people would suppose him to
be a prominent Roman church official of that name.[2]

Macabiau's petitions grew out of the three earlier petitions
submitted to the Vatican Council in 1870. Two of these,
signed respectively by 118 bishops and 43 superiors-general
of religious orders, asked that St. Joseph be granted special
honors in the liturgy, and that he be proclaimed Patron of
the Universal Church. The third petition more specifically
asked that St. Joseph be proclaimed Patron of the Universal

Church, and also that the cultus of *protodulia* be granted him. The list of signers was impressive: 38 cardinals of the 42 at the Council, including the future Leo XIII, and 217 patriarchs, primates, archbishops, and bishops. Their petition did not use the precise word *protodulia* but read, "The public cultus of *dulia,* second to the Blessed Mother and before all other saints." This concept came to be called *protodulia,* that is, "first veneration," to parallel the *hyperdulia* given our Blessed Lady.

By way of digression, we must explain that the insistence of some theologians that St. Joseph be given a *protodulia* specifically superior to the veneration given other saints seems to have been an obstacle hindering further honors for St. Joseph. The final word on the subject must come from the Holy See in case a decision ever becomes necessary. The important fact to be remembered is that Joseph's cultus, whether called *protodulia* or by any other name, must not imply his intrinsic co-operation in the Incarnation of our Lord. Mary alone accomplished this.[3] However, it is striking to note that the Church now ranks St. Joseph second to Mary in many recent prayers, and Leo XIII's oft-quoted words in *Quamquam Pluries* clearly designate Joseph as second to Mary in dignity. Hence, it seems that the Holy See does not wish to be involved in any way in deciding whether Joseph's veneration is to be specifically or merely quantitatively superior to that of other saints. In practice, St. Joseph is now given a rank second only to Mary.

As it eventuated, the Vatican Council did not act on the petitions submitted to it, but Pius IX responded by proclaiming St. Joseph Patron of the Universal Church. Nothing further was done concerning the request for *protodulia* until Macabiau took up the matter in 1887. He amplified the original petition of 1870, and sent it for signatures to 900 prelates of the Latin rite. Of these, no fewer than 632 cardinals and bishops — among them the future St. Pius X — gave their support. Meanwhile, Leo XIII issued his monu-

mental encyclical on St. Joseph, the greatest pronouncement
of the Church concerning the Saint. The outlook for new
honors was, therefore, bright indeed when there suddenly
appeared the decree of August 15, 1892. This action of the
Congregation of Sacred Rites indicated that the Holy See
wished no changes at the time. The wording of the decree
should be noted carefully. It does not criticize the soundness
of the theological doctrine on which the petitions for St.
Joseph's advancement rested. There is only the question
whether or not a change at that time is expedient:

"From all sides petitions have been sent to the Apostolic
See, asking that St. Joseph be honored in the sacred liturgy
with a cultus of higher rank. His Holiness was filled with the
greatest joy because of these supplications which were presented to him . . . nevertheless he did not think fit to bestow
on the holy Patriarch a higher liturgical cultus which would
alter the status wisely established in the Church over a long
period."[4]

Evidently because of this decree Macabiau withheld his
petition, deeming it prudent to await a more propitious
moment. In 1908 he finally published it in amplified book
form addressed to Pope St. Pius X and entitled, *De Cultu
Sancti Josephi Amplificando* — "On Advancing the Cultus
of St. Joseph." The first part of his petition was practically
the same as that of the 1870 request for *protodulia*. To it was
added a second section which asked "that the venerable name
of Joseph, as the supreme Patron of the Universal Church,
second to the Mother of God, should be invoked in the
Sacrifice of the Mass, namely, in the *Confiteor* and in the
prayers *Suscipe, Sancta Trinitas, Communicantes,* and *Libera
Nos,* following the most sweet name of Mary."[5]

We can now enter on a study of the nature of this request.
Again the fact must be underlined that the decision on these
changes rests wholly within the competence of the Holy See.
Promoters of these petitions have been loyal and obedient
Catholics who have wished to submit to the authority of the

Holy Father at all times. Usually, however, the pope decides a question after the theologians and historians have discussed freely the pros and cons. In this spirit we offer the following data, not necessarily as a thoroughly original contribution but as a cumulative summary of the monographs that have been published on the subject. Particularly represented here are the thoughts of Macabiau.

REASONS AGAINST THE CHANGES

Strong objections have been brought forward against making the changes suggested in the petitions. Some theologians claimed that since Joseph died before the Passion of our Lord, it would not be fitting in the mystical sacrifice of the Cross to invoke a saint whose death preceded Calvary. Others have said that only those who shed their blood for Christ should be invoked in the important prayers of the Mass, and this reasoning would exclude St. Joseph, who was both patriarch and confessor. Finally, the approbation of such a novelty as "greatly unessential additions" (as Jungmann characterizes them in his work on the Mass)[6] might open the way to claims for all sorts of saints. Venerated age-old traditions should not be recklessly flaunted. Above all, so the arguments run, such a change would be against the mind of the Church. In 1815 Pius VII did not see fit to grant a request to place St. Joseph's name in the Canon of the Mass. The 1892 decree of the Congregation of Sacred Rites made it clear that Leo XIII disapproved of tampering with the long-standing traditions of the Roman Mass.

Even in times closer to our day, these objections have continued. Dom Gaston Démaret, O.S.B., wrote in 1939, "To modify, even to embellish and to enrich the ancient formulae of the liturgy is something repugnant to Rome. It is very circumspect . . . and the Ordinary of the Mass and especially the Canon are for her the holy arch which no one is permitted to touch. One adds nothing, not even a stone which would decorate it, to the masterpiece which has come down

to us from antiquity. It would be a sort of profanation." He
adds that since St. Gregory the Great the Canon has "under-
gone no modification or addition of any sort," and it was for
this reason that Dom Couturier, successor of Dom Gueranger
refused to sign Macabiau's petition at Solesmes, despite his
tender and confident devotion to St. Joseph.[7]

EVIDENCE FOR THE CHANGES

As is manifest, the two rejections of the petitions by the
Church were for the moment, and did not necessarily prevent
renewed petitions in the future. As for the objections against
St. Joseph as a saint of the Old Testament, they might with
equal reason be directed against Abraham or Melchisedech,
who also are mentioned in the Canon of the Mass! Actually,
the many objections reduce to one valid principle: Age-old
tradition should be respected. In the case of St. Joseph's
petitions the principle still holds. Customs handed down
through the centuries should not be changed without a grave
reason. In this instance such a grave reason seems to exist.
By the providence of God St. Joseph was not explicitly honored in the Mass in past times. In our own day because of
changed circumstances one might have reason to think that
the moment for his full public veneration is arriving. What
are the positive data that urge such a step?

First of all, there is the fact of St. Joseph's dignity. The
Church now teaches and in practice venerates the Saint as
second only to Mary. Hence, corresponding honor should be
paid him in the Church's supreme act of worship. No one
today denies that St. Joseph's name would have been listed
directly after that of our Lady if the Canon of the Mass had
been composed in our own time. In Jungmann's study of
the origins of the Mass, the author (who seems to show himself unsympathetic to the changes) admits that "under Leo
XIII because of a French petition it was an almost accomplished fact that the name of St. Joseph was to be added in
the *Confiteor, Suscipe S. Trinitas, Communicantes,* and

Libera Nos."[8] It can even be said that this insertion would probably have been made long ago if the Saint's excellence had been explicitly recognized in the days of the Mass's composition.

The argument from consideration of Joseph's dignity gains in force when we consider the dignity of other saints of the Mass. In the case of most of them we do not know exactly why their names were included in the Canon in preference to all others. Perhaps it was because of their connection with the early Church or because of their martyrdom or because the faithful at Rome honored their memory with particular devotion. At the time their names were listed in the Mass prayers, the chief cause for this action was a desire to show them honor. Throughout all Christian centuries this mention in the Canon was looked upon as a great mark of recognized dignity. The same principle, it seems, should hold for St. Joseph.

As for the objection that the Saint is not sufficiently linked with the Sacrifice of the Mass, only one answer need be given: a forthright denial. Next to the Blessed Virgin no one more than St. Joseph co-operated in preparing for the Redemption. Jesus took His human nature within the bonds of Joseph's virginal marriage to our Lady, and this was a necessary prelude according to God's plans. Jesus was reared to full manhood by St. Joseph. This vocation of Joseph was directly chosen by God to fit into the divine plan of the Redemption also. Finally, the fact of Joseph's holiness shows how generously the Saint united himself to Mary's offering, so that the two parents of Jesus were one in purpose with their Son. The lack of martyrdom by sword or by fire should not harm Joseph's privilege to be closely associated with the Mass of the Martyrs any more than the absence of physical martyrdom fails to detract from the glory of Mary's title of Queen of Martyrs.

Joseph's intimacy with Mary brings to mind another thought that he be linked with her in the Mass as well. As a general rubric, SS. Peter and Paul are not to be separated when liturgical honors are paid one or the other. How much more compelling is the reason for the names of Mary and Joseph, virginal wife and virginal husband and virginal parents of Jesus, to be at least *occasionally* united in the greatest act of communal worship in Christ's Church!

Joseph's relationship to the Church affords the most pertinent and most pressing of all grounds that he should be recognized in the Mass. At the impulse of the Holy Spirit the Church proclaimed St. Joseph its special and universal Patron. A universal patron, however, should be invoked by all his clients in all fitting circumstances. No occasion is more fitting than the Church's supreme act of sacrifice and prayer. If St. Joseph's name is not included in the prayers of the Mass, it would appear that the Church had proclaimed for itself a patron saint whom it does not invoke on the most proper occasion, or a patron whom it does not invoke while it is paying honor to many minor and obscure saints.

Again and again in history additions were made to the Mass on the occasion of growing evils. If ever any century in the world's history called for special help from God to fight the forces of evil, certainly the present one does so. Pius IX's declaration of St. Joseph as Patron of the Universal Church was to a great extent prompted by the dire need of Joseph's aid. Pius XI declared the Saint patron to help the Church fight atheistic communism. Leo XIII and Benedict XV pointed out how devotion to Mary and devotion to Joseph go hand in hand. Ought not St. Joseph be invoked proportionately?

The question of adding the name of the Saint to the prayers of the Mass does not incur any difficulty as far as the dogmas of the Church are concerned. The rites of the Church — and particularly the Latin Mass — have been changed in the past by Roman Pontiffs, and can be changed now. Such additions or revisions are thoroughly within the power of the popes.

A MASS UNCHANGED FROM ANTIQUITY?

One possibly serious difficulty calls for fuller discussion. Have the rites of the Mass been handed down to us unchanged from antiquity? The answer is that the Mass has been static only since the time of Pope St. Pius V (that is from the second half of the sixteenth century). Many changes were made in Mass prayers during the Middle Ages. Bover, relying on Batiffol, says, "Anyone who would think that the modern Mass formulary was compiled in its entirety by St. Gregory I would be in grievous error."[9] Some of these changes can be listed briefly here:

a) The *Confiteor* was not recited in the Mass before the tenth or eleventh century. During the Middle Ages innumerable formulae of the prayer were used, and it was only in the fourteenth century that the names of St. Michael and St. John the Baptist were added to those of the Apostles Peter and Paul.[10]

b) In the case of the *Suscipe Sancta Trinitas* the prayer itself did not come into common use until the eleventh century, and even then its formula was not the one recited today.[11]

c) The prayer of the Canon, *Communicantes,* offers need for the greatest reverence as the most ancient of the prayers under discussion. It seems to have been edited by Gregory the Great at the end of the sixth century. Hence, the prayer now recited is not the primitive Roman formula.[12] Not only was its catalog of saints changed throughout the centuries; during the Middle Ages it was an approved practice to insert the name of the saint whose feast was celebrated or whose relics were reserved in the Church where Mass was being offered.[13]

d) As for the *Libera Nos, Quaesumus,* as late as the eleventh century a rubric permitted the priest to substitute after the name of St. Andrew any or as many names of other saints as he wished to mention. In this as well as in the pre-

ceding prayer we have mentioned, no universal invocation
of John the Baptist occurred.[14]

THE LITANY OF THE SAINTS

Any discussion of the arguments for placing Joseph's name
into the prayers of the Mass naturally borders on the related
petitions for the Saint's preferment in the Litany of the
Saints. Because of the antiquity of this litany — it dates from
the early days of the Church — the prayer was strongly influenced by the opinion of its times that St. Joseph should be
kept in the background lest his unique position be misunderstood and imperil the doctrines pertaining to Christ and
to Mary. It was only after 1726 that the Saint's name was
officially inserted into the Litany of the Saints, and even then
it was placed after the archangels, the angels, and St. John
the Baptist. St. Joseph apparently had been included in the
litany in many places after Bologna set the example for other
localities to follow in or about 1350.

But Joseph's name was dropped at some time during the
sixteenth century — no record exists to explain precisely why.
The most plausible explanation is given by Cardinal Prosper
Lambertini, the scholar who later became Benedict XIV.
After the reformation of the Roman Breviary in the pontificate of St. Pius V, he writes, the invocation of St. Joseph was
no longer mentioned in the Greater Litanies, even though
it is listed in such litanies printed in missals before this
period. Evidently, he concludes, this omission was made because of the ignorance of the printers. They had been in-
formed that the proper Office of St. Joseph was suppressed
by Pius V; and on their own authority they went ahead and
deleted St. Joseph's name from the Greater Litanies.

Four reasons exist to justify this conclusion: first, these
same printers *added* saints' names at their own whim to the
litanies. Second, no decree can be discovered prohibiting St.
Joseph's invocation; third, no plausible reason can be found

to explain why Pius V would even wish to omit St. Joseph's name. Finally, a later pope, Paul V, confirmed and approved litanies for the blessing of holy water, as these were inserted in the *Roman Ritual*. In these the invocation of St. Joseph was mentioned. Hence, we have additional proof that the Holy See never ordered the Saint's name deleted.[15]

The hundreds of Catholic bishops who in the past petitioned the Holy See to place Joseph's name second to Mary, eventually had their request admirably seconded by the approval of the Litany of St. Joseph, the Preface of St. Joseph, and the invocation of St. Joseph in the Divine Praises and in the prayers for the dying. These exclusive honors have led many prelates to believe that the Church will in time accord St. Joseph an equally significant position in the Litany of the Saints, directly following the invocation of our Lady.

Marchesi's suggestions, like those he made for St. Joseph in the Mass (p. 95 ff.), are as follows:

"Lord, have mercy on us, Christ, have mercy on us, etc.," to: "Holy Mary, pray for us; Holy Mother of God, pray for us; Holy Virgin of virgins, pray for us"; here he would insert: "Saint Joseph, pray for us; Spouse of the Virgin Mother, pray for us; Loving parents of Christ, pray for us."[16] He adds that if misunderstanding were feared, the last title might be changed to "loving *virginal* parents of Christ." Then would follow the invocation of St. Michael, St. Gabriel, St. Raphael, and the angels; next, St. John the Baptist alone would be saluted before the invocation of all prophets and patriarchs, since St. Joseph in this arrangement would be moved next to Mary, as part of the Holy Family instead of being one of the patriarchs. But for what the future may exactly bring, we need only note that the arguments for St. Joseph's advance in the Litany of the Saints coincide with the reasons for his inclusion in the prayers of the Mass.

At this point, the following summary condenses the data offered into the following statements:

1. The difficulty of *rigid* antiquity of the prayers in question does not exist;

2. The popes have the authority to make the change;

3. The change would be anything but drastic — merely the relocating of one or two invocations in the Litany of the Saints, perhaps an addition of one or two titles to St. Joseph; and the addition of four words, "St. Joseph, her spouse," in four prayers of the Mass. Yet the question remains: Since the requests were twice refused, in 1815 and in 1892, how may devout Catholics continue to hope that the Holy See will make an alteration?

The actions of the Holy See are the best answer. At the time when the first petitions were presented, historical facts which are now admitted concerning the origins of the Mass had not yet been ascertained. Moreover, it must be conceded in all fairness that the doctrines held by some of the promoters of the petitions came close to exaggerating the limits of St. Joseph's magnificence, perhaps even infringing on the dignity of Mary or that of the eternal Father. Above all, the Church acts with the utmost caution and prudence, knowing that it is always guided by the Holy Spirit. In God's own time, if the changes in the Mass are to be made in St. Joseph's favor, these will be brought about by the legitimate channels which God in His well-ordered providence will use. It is most striking that the Church has given St. Joseph equivalently all honors requested by early petitioners *except* this final honor of placing the Saint's name in the Mass. In fact, the Church has gone much farther than requested. St. Joseph has been given two feasts of exclusive rank and distinction. The Church had been asked to declare his veneration one of *protodulia,* but instead of making the explicit declaration in such a way as to settle a theological controversy, the Church in practice venerates Joseph after Mary. Such is the tenor of the decrees of Pius IX, of Leo XIII's encyclical, and of the changes in the Church's public prayers we have already noted.

MEDIATOR DEI

Up to this point we have presented the substance of arguments advanced since 1870 to the present. One is surprised to compare the principles on which they are based with the principles set forth in *Mediator Dei,* the great encyclical of Pius XII issued in 1947 concerning the liturgy, and to find how much they agree:

1. In the first place, Pius indicates that the liturgy is not static but is susceptible of proper growth: "The Sacred Liturgy does in fact include divine as well as human elements. The former, instituted as they have been by God, cannot be changed in any way by men. But the human components admit of various modifications, as the needs of the age, circumstances, and the good of souls may require, and as the ecclesiastical hierarchy under guidance of the Holy Spirit may have authorized."[17]

2. The Pope further explains that some of these human elements in the liturgy have developed because of disciplinary modifications, a more explicit formulation of doctrine, the development of the fine arts, and nonliturgical practices. Here he mentions the part of the devotions "which began to appear by God's wonderful design in later periods and grew to be so popular. We may instance the spread and ever mounting ardor of devotion to the Blessed Eucharist, devotion to the most bitter Passion of our Redeemer, devotion to the most Sacred Heart of Jesus, to the Virgin Mother of God, and to her most chaste spouse."[18]

3. The Holy Father clearly disapproves of exaggerated attachment to ancient rites and excessive archaism: "Ancient usage must not be esteemed more suitable and proper, either in its own right or in its significance for later times and new situations, on the simple ground that it carries the savor and aroma of antiquity. . . . It is neither wise nor laudable to reduce everything to antiquity by every possible device."[19]

4. Finally, changes are on no account to be made accord-

ing to private judgment: "The Sovereign Pontiff alone enjoys the right to recognize and establish any practice touching the worship of God, to introduce and approve new rites, as also to modify those he judges to require modification."[20]

It is on this note of filial obedience to the Vicar of Christ that we close this chapter on the petitions for St. Joseph's advance in the liturgy. Words used elsewhere seem equally fitting to be used again in closing this book: "We may hope to see the day when the Holy Father will judge it opportune to climax centuries of growing esteem and love by placing the foster father of Jesus Christ next to his immaculate spouse in the greatest liturgical act of the Church. Is not this a worthy object of our prayers?"[21]

REFERENCES — CHAPTER SIX

1. Aloysius Marchesi, *Amplificationis Cultus Sancti Josephi B.M.V. Sponsi* (Rome: Marietti, 1870), II, c. 6, art. 2, 238.

2. M. F. Cavallera, S.J., in *Revue d'ascétique et de Mystique*, 24 (1948), 295–296.

3. Michel, *DTC*, 8, 1520.

4. *Authent. Collect. S.R.C.*, Decr. 3789.

5. Macabiau, 16.

6. Josef Andreas Jungmann, S.J., *Missarum Sollemnia* (Vienna: Herder, 1948), 1, 212.

7. Gaston Démaret, O.S.B., *Marie de qui est né Jésus*, Paris, 1939, tom. 6, 339.

8. Jungmann, 1, 212.

9. Bover, 56.

10. Jungmann, 2, 375.

11. *Ibid.*, 2, 56.

12. *Ibid.*, 2, 214.

13. *Ibid.*, 2, 215.

14. *Ibid.*, 2, 346.

15. Cardinal Lambertini's report to the Congregation of Sacred Rites is printed in *SI* 2854–2881. Cf. *SI* 2866 for his hypothesis on printers' omissions.

16. Marchesi, II, 9, 241.

17. Pius XII, *Mediator Dei*, November 20, 1947, *AAS* 39, 521; par. 50 of NCWC ed., Vat. Lib. tr.

18. *Ibid.*, par. 54.

19. *Ibid.*, par. 61, 62, 63.

20. *Ibid.*, par. 58.

21. *MNC*, 192.

Devotion to St. Joseph During the Past 400 Years

IN THE RELIGIOUS ORDERS

AFTER the Council of Trent (1545–1563) the religious orders continued to propagate the devotion to St. Joseph and to place themselves under St. Joseph's protection just as they had done during the early stages of the devotion. In addition to the orders that had played important parts in obtaining recognition for the Saint — e.g., Benedictines, Carmelites, Dominicans, Franciscans, and the Servites — new ones sprang up that adopted the devotion wholeheartedly. Among these the Society of Jesus from its very beginning in 1534 made the veneration of St. Joseph almost an inborn characteristic. St. Ignatius of Loyola, its founder, held up the members of the Holy Family to his spiritual sons as the exemplars of paternal authority and filial obedience,[1] and in his golden book of the *Spiritual Exercises,* one of the most potent instruments of reform in the Church, Ignatius introduced St. Joseph into the gospel meditations on the early life of our Lord. Jesuit devotion to the Holy Family probably grew out of the strong love for the person of Christ which Ignatius inculcated into his followers.

Jesuit influence showed itself most influentially in the case of theologians like Alphonsus Salmeron, St. Peter Canisius, and Cornelius a Lapide. Above all others, Francis Suarez

(† 1617) revolutionized the theological treatment of the Saint
by describing Joseph as a member of the "order of the
hypostatic union" — in other words, picturing the Saint as an
intimate co-operator in the redemptive work of Jesus with
Mary. According to Sommervogel's encyclopedic catalogue of
Jesuit writers, more than 130 independent works on St.
Joseph were published by Jesuits after 1600.

During the last half of the sixteenth century the Carmelite
foundress, St. Teresa of Avila, brought St. Joseph's cause to
the forefront in Spain, so that even outside the cloisters of
her order, the devotion became strongly ingrained in the
Catholic life of the country. The well-known passage from
the sixth chapter of Teresa's *Autobiography* has often been
quoted as one of the most excellent descriptions of Joseph's
intercessory power and affectionate protection. (See p. 93.)
However, this is not the only record of Joseph's influence in
the life of Teresa.

"One day after Communion," she wrote, "our Lord commanded me to labor with all my might for this end . . .
[promising] that the monastery would certainly be built . . .
that it should be called St. Joseph's; and that St. Joseph
would keep guard at one door and our Lady at the other;
that Christ would be in the midst of us."

Again, "Once, when I was in one of my difficulties, not
knowing what to do and unable to pay the workmen, my true
father and lord St. Joseph appeared to me, and gave me to
understand that money would not be wanting; and I must
hire the workmen."

Teresa's devotion to the Saint appears most of all in the
story of her great vision. Here, too, is a dramatization of
Joseph's role close to Mary. "On one of these days . . . I fell
into so profound a trance that I was, as it were, beside
myself . . . I thought, then, when I was in that state that
I saw myself clothed with a garment of excessive whiteness
and splendor. At first I did not see who was putting it on me.
Afterwards I saw our Lady on my right hand, and my father

St. Joseph on my left, clothing me with that garment. I was given to understand that I was then cleansed from my sins.

"When I had been thus clad (I was filled with the utmost delight and joy), our Lady seemed at once to take me by both hands. She said that I pleased her very much by being devout to the glorious St. Joseph; that I might rely on it that my desires about the monastery would be accomplished; and that our Lord and they, too, would be greatly honored in it; that I was to be afraid of no failure whatever . . . because they would watch over us and because her Son had promised to be with us. . . . I did not see St. Joseph so distinctly, though I saw clearly that he was there."[2]

Of the seventeen monasteries which she founded, Teresa dedicated twelve to St. Joseph. Her writings were most influential; and her spirit of devotion to the Saint lived vigorously in her order. After her death the general chapter of the Carmelite Fathers selected St. Joseph as patron of the order. This occurred in 1621. A more momentous event took place in 1680. The Carmelites obtained permission to celebrate the feast of the Patronage of St. Joseph on the third Sunday after Easter. Here we see the origins of the Solemnity of St. Joseph, the feast that honored the Saint's universal patronage until it was replaced by the feast of Joseph the Worker in 1956.

In 1632 the Hermits of St. Augustine had placed all their Italian and German establishments under the protection of St. Joseph. Later, in 1700, they, too, were allowed to celebrate the feast of the Patronage, together with the additional privilege of making a liturgical commemoration of the Saint in every office of "semidouble" rank.

Francis de Sales and Vincent de Paul also deserve mention as moving spirits in the further growth of the devotion. Vincent made the Saint patron of his seminaries; Francis chose Joseph as patron of the Visitation Order which he had founded, and urged his spiritual daughters to imitate Joseph closely. The influence of De Sales worked most powerfully for St. Joseph in the tributes of his book, *On the Love of God,* and in the nineteenth of his *Spiritual Conferences,* which presented solid theological analysis in a devotional format. We have already quoted St. Francis in ranking St. Joseph after our Lady in perfection and holiness (p. 53); it is in this same "Nineteenth Conference" that de Sales showed Joseph's union with Jesus through the marriage to our Lady:

"By means of the marriage between our Lady and the glorious St. Joseph, the Good of eternal goods, our Lord Himself, belonged to St. Joseph as well as to our Lady. This is not true as regards the nature which he took in the womb of our glorious mistress, and which had been formed by the Holy Spirit of the most pure blood of our Lady; but it is true as regards grace, which made him participate in all the possessions of his beloved spouse and which increased so marvellously his growth in perfection; and this through his continual communication with our Lady."[3]

The history of the devotion to St. Joseph in the Order of the Visitation becomes that of almost all orders and could be continued at great length. Hundreds of monasteries and convents have been named in honor of him and have been consecrated to him as the special exemplar and protector of their members. Since a detailed list would run into large numbers, the over-all impression can best be obtained by mentioning a few of these religious families, but particularly those that bear the name of St. Joseph.

In a certain sense the very existence of congregations such as these has been a mighty stimulus to honor the Saint. It is true that their members privately honored their patron; but the exterior works they accomplished as well as their selfless dedication to so many varied apostolates have served to call attention to the man whose closeness to Jesus and to Mary has been their inspiration. Some of these foundations are now extinct, such as the Cretenists or "Missionaries of St. Joseph" which the physician, J. Cretenet, began in Lyons, France, about 1650. Another group, the "Knights of St. Joseph," was reorganized in 1807 in Tuscany and was based on a brotherhood of St. Joseph that had first existed at Florence in 1514. Victor Emanuel, however, suppressed these Knights later in the nineteenth century.

Perhaps the most striking, because of its numbers and because of the eventual world-wide extent of its work, has been the Congregation of the Sisters of St. Joseph. The group was founded at Le Puy, France, in 1650 by Bishop Henri de Maupas and Jean-Pierre Medaille, S.J. It was based on the Rule of St. Augustine and the original principles of Francis de Sales, devoting itself to works of mercy and to education. At the present day at least 25,000 Sisters of St. Joseph are working for Christ in this organization whose name and history have constantly served to remind the world of the head of the Holy Family.

A full enumeration of the religious families dedicated by name to St. Joseph offers the following interesting list:

five groups of men are no longer in existence;

six priests' congregations are now flourishing, of which the best known in the United States is St. Joseph's Society of the Sacred Heart, for Colored Missions;

three religious brotherhoods of St. Joseph;

three women's orders of St. Joseph; and

eleven women's congregations in whose title the Saint's name appears.

But the picture is still incomplete. Nine associations for lay people exist in the Church as archconfraternities, unions, etc. Among them is the Pious Union of St. Joseph's Passing, founded for the benefit of all who are in their last agony.[4] Thus, the head of the Holy Family has truly become the head of numerous religious families, just as in countless individual cases husbands and wives have chosen Joseph's love of Jesus and Mary to be the spirit that reigns at their hearth.

THE DEVOTION TO ST. JOSEPH
IN EUROPE

After the century of the Council of Trent and the Protestant Revolt, the 1600's witnessed official public honor for St. Joseph in many countries of Europe. These were, of course, the so-called Catholic countries, for in lands where persecution raged, such public devotion was out of the question.

Quite remarkable signs of esteem for the Saint were manifested. Ferdinand III in 1655 wished St. Joseph to be proclaimed as the special patron of the kingdom of Bohemia under the title of "Preserver of the Peace." Ferdinand's son, Leopold I, publicly turned to the intercession of the Saint in order to obtain from God the favor of male succession. Meanwhile, he declared Joseph patron of all Austria. When the Emperor's first son was born, he gratefully named him Joseph even though this name had hitherto never been used in any European dynasty. It was in this way that the name of St. Joseph was to be connected (through a later Joseph) with an anticlerical political system.

The most critical event in Leopold's reign was the Turkish menace to Europe. In 1683 the Turks were beaten off by the generalship of John Sobieski at Vienna, and later they were completely vanquished. Leopold attributed the Vienna victory to St. Joseph's protection, and on February 5, 1684, wrote to Pope Innocent XI on this score:

"When the whole Christian world stood in peril because of the siege of Vienna, the struggle which led to the defeat of the Turkish hordes began on the heights of Kahlenberg ("Bald Mountain"), dedicated to St. Joseph. The outcome seems to show that our merciful God, moved by the intercession of this patron and protector, wished to grant this manifold victory to His people.

"Accordingly, since we think it fitting and just that the veneration and devotion to the most holy patriarch, foster father of the Son of God and spouse of the ever pure Virgin Mary, should daily increase, we beg Your Holiness with childlike confidence to grant our petition: that the name of the holy patriarch Joseph be included in the Litany of the Saints, and that the feast of his Patronage, as the Discalced Carmelite Fathers have long possessed it and celebrate it on the third Sunday after Easter, be prescribed as a universal feast."[5]

The petition was not successful. There was fear at Rome of starting an unwelcome precedent in changing the Litany of the Saints. As for a feast of thanksgiving, the results of our Lady's intercession showed prominently in the victory over the Moslems and should have been commemorated before all else. Hence, Innocent XI extended to the whole Church the feast of the Most Holy Name of Mary, and did not see fit to grant Leopold's request. Instead, the Emperor's dominions were given special permission to celebrate the feast of the Espousal of Joseph and Mary. This was in gratitude to God not only for the conquest at Vienna but also for the succeeding battles in Hungary which permanently broke the Turkish power.

Innocent XI likewise granted the feast of the Espousal to Spain. Spanish devotion to St. Joseph was so strong that Charles II petitioned the pope to declare the Saint patron of Spain. This declaration was made in 1689, but a tempest of criticism was aroused because the decree which granted the petition was not made out in proper form. In addition, the opposing faction claimed that the traditional position of St. James as patron of Spain had been impugned. As a result of these protests, in 1690 the declaration of St. Joseph as patron of Spain was pronounced null and void as if it had never been issued.

The entire incident is unfortunate, to say the least; but the reaction against the decree as well as the subsequent revocation does not reflect any lack of zeal on the part of the Spanish people in general, who have clung to the devotion to

St. Joseph with a long-traditional enthusiasm. There seems to be no Spanish name more common than "José." Leo XIII's letter of 1890, restoring the feast of St. Joseph in Spanish lands to its pristine dignity, pays lavish tribute to this devotion. A letter of the same pope, written a few months later, avers that Portugal is no less devout to the Saint.[6]

It was because of the Spanish petition of Charles II that Belgium came to be placed under the patronage of St. Joseph. At the time of the request, in 1679, the Spanish possessions included most of what is now Belgium. When the Spanish clergy, wishing to keep St. James as patron of Spain, protested against the grant of the Holy See concerning St. Joseph, the Congregation of Sacred Rites nullified the decree, but only in so far as it concerned Spain, not for the possessions of Spain. Hence, the invalidation did not take effect in Belgium, where the original announcement had been received with popular joy and acclaim.[7]

The Germany of the seventeenth century was a war-torn land, but despite its tragic conditions, we can discern some indication of the regard of the faithful for St. Joseph. For example, in 1661 the Prince-Bishop Bernard von Galen obtained papal permission to consecrate his entire diocese to the Saint. This followed upon the Bishop's triumphal reentry into Münster on July 7, 1661, when the silver statue of St. Joseph was carried in solemn procession. A synod of 1662 directed the local clergy to spread the love and knowledge of the Saint among the people, and especially to preach his powerful intercession as the patron of a happy death.

In France, Father Pierre Coton (Cotton), S.J. († 1626), was one of the most active proponents of the devotion in all its history. From 1603 to 1617, Coton worked both at the Court and among the people for the cause of his friend and heavenly patron. Coton was a versatile and brilliant preacher and controversialist, who used all the influence he could muster for the cause of St. Joseph. Partly as the result of his work, on June 20, 1613, Marie de Medici personally laid the cornerstone of what is believed to be the first church of St. Joseph on French soil. This was the church of the Discalced Carmelites in Paris, completed in 1620 and solemnly consecrated on December 21, 1625.

At about the same time, due to Coton's efforts the new Jesuit church at Lyons was also dedicated to the Saint. In Paris, a group of Reformed Cistercians known as the Feuillants also made this dedication of their church "to the spread and grateful recognition of the excellence of incomparable St. Joseph." Here, in 1657 this church of the Feuillants witnessed Bossuet's matchless "First Panegyric" preached on St. Joseph. Bossuet was only in his thirty-first year, but his oratorical genius was shown so plainly that he was commanded to repeat his panegyric in 1659 before the Queen Mother, Anne of Austria, as well as her company. In addition to this double rendition of the "First Panegyric," Bossuet delivered a second such sermon in the Lent of 1661.

Anne's devotion to St. Joseph was well known, and Bossuet's oratory thus wakened a desire at the French court to have the general observance of the feast of St. Joseph extended to France. Even so worldly a monarch as Louis XIV expressed a wish to that effect. Pope Gregory XV had prescribed the feast as a holyday of obligation in 1621, and Urban VIII had repeated the directive in 1642, but it still had not been carried out in France. Hence, Coton and Bossuet had to overcome much indifference regarding St. Joseph.

Bossuet's first panegyric on the Saint is called the *Depositum Custodi,* from the text, "Guard the trust" (1 Tim. 6:20). The oration elaborates the three trusts committed to Joseph's care: the virginity of Mary, the rearing of Jesus Christ, and the secret of the Incarnation. Certain sections of the sermon merit our attention here, as examples of Bossuet's description of Joseph's vocation.

"Can we confirm in more express terms the truth which I preach?" Bossuet asks. "You behold the dignity of Mary in the fact that her blessed virginity has been chosen from eternity to give Jesus Christ to the world; and you behold the dignity of Joseph in the fact that this purity of Mary, which has been of such value to our nature, has been confided to his care. It is he who preserves for the world something so needful. O Joseph, 'guard the trust!' Guard dearly this sacred trust of Mary's purity. Since it has pleased the Eternal Father to protect Mary's virginity under the veil of this marriage, she can no longer preserve it without you; and thus your purity has become in a fashion necessary for the world, by the glorious charge which has been given you to protect the purity of Mary. . . ."

"But it is not enough for the Eternal Father to have confided to Joseph the virginity of Mary. He prepares for him something even more exalted; and after having entrusted to his loyalty this holy virginity which is to give Jesus Christ to the world (as if He planned to exhaust His infinite generosity in favor of the Patriarch), He is now about to place Jesus Christ Himself into Joseph's hands, and He wishes him protected by Joseph's care. If we penetrate into this secret, if we enter into the depths of this mystery, O faithful people, there it is that we shall discover something so glorious for the just man Joseph that we will never be able to understand it sufficiently! . . ."

"Among all vocations, I discern two in the Scriptures which seem diametrically opposed. The first is that of the apostles; the second, that of Joseph. Jesus is revealed to the apostles, Jesus is revealed to Joseph, but under very contrary conditions. He is revealed to the apostles in order to be proclaimed throughout the entire world; He is revealed to Joseph in order to be in silence and to be hidden. The apostles are lights to make Jesus Christ visible to the world; Joseph is a veil to cover Him; and under this mysterious veil, there is hidden the virginity of Mary and the magnificence of the Savior of souls. . . . The holy apostles preach the Gospel so valiantly that the sound of their preaching reaches even unto heaven. Joseph on the contrary, hearing the story of the marvels of Jesus Christ, listens, admires, and is silent."[8]

But we must return to the course of the devotion in other countries of Europe. In Rome the guild of masons and carpenters dedicated a new church to the Saint in 1596, in the fifty-eighth year of the guild's existence. Annually, on the feast day, the poor or the orphaned daughters of guild members received a dowry from the common funds. Also on this day, a condemned criminal might receive pardon by reason of an indult of Gregory XIII. In 1598 a certain Desiderius, Canon of the Church of St. Mary of the Martyrs (the ancient pagan pantheon), organized a pious union of painters, architects, and other artists in honor of St. Joseph. A chapel was erected in the church, and the altar consecrated to the Saint. Every March 19, this association like its fellow guild presented a destitute maiden with a fitting dowry. Such a predilection of the guilds for St. Joseph appeared in Belgium and France as well as at Rome. The guild at Antwerp, for instance, possessed its own chapel in the cathedral, dedicating the altar there to St. Joseph.

These, then, represent some of the marks of the devotion to St. Joseph in the Europe of the seventeenth century. During the ominous eighteenth century, the situation of the Church grew steadily worse; and in common with the temporal misfortunes of the Church, the devotion to the Saint seems to have remained stagnant as far as public marks of honor were concerned. Only with the reign of Pius IX (beginning in 1846, when we are already in touch with the modern phase of the devotion) does that new vigor appear which has culminated in our present-day recognition of the Saint.

As for the devotional and theological literature of the period after the Council of Trent, literally hundreds of essays and independent works were published concerning St. Joseph's vocation. The great names of Suarez, Cornelius

a Lapide, Francis de Sales, Teresa of Avila, and Bossuet are
already familiar to us. In addition to these, several others
also deserve mention. Prosper Lambertini (the future Benedict XIV) sponsored, as we shall later tell, the inclusion of
St. Joseph's name in the Litany of the Saints. Father Joseph
Patrignani, S.J., was the author of a biography of St. Joseph,
a devotional work that first appeared in 1709 and then became one of the most widely reprinted and translated books
ever written concerning the Saint. St. Alphonsus Liguori
(† 1787), bishop, founder of the Redemptorists, and Doctor
of the Church, was responsible for a series of meditations
and sermons that faithfully reflect a candid theological appraisal of St. Joseph and his service to our Lord and our
Lady. After Liguori's century, the English convert, Father
Frederick William Faber († 1863) gave to the world a warm
appreciation of St. Joseph in his several volumes, particularly
in *Bethlehem* and *The Blessed Sacrament*. Faber's writings
were all the more valuable because their author drew co-
piously on dogmatic theology, while presenting his subject in
inspiring devotional language.

DEVOTION TO ST. JOSEPH ON THE MISSIONS

It would be a huge task to give an adequate presentation
of the strength and influence of the devotion to St. Joseph
in the mission fields of the Church during the seventeenth
and eighteenth centuries. North America, Paraguay, India,
and China all witnessed the self-sacrifice of missionaries who
dedicated their work to the head of the Holy Family. We can
illustrate this fervor by beginning with the story of the North
American martyrs and their companions: John de Brebeuf,
Isaac Jogues, LeJeune, Lallemant.

In trying to teach and convert the Indians, the missionaries
used all possible means to make the Faith attractive and
colorful to savage minds throttled by brutality and supersti-
tion. One of the methods the Fathers found useful was the

celebration of the feasts of Jesus, Mary, and Joseph in grand style. Primarily, of course, they wished to pay homage to the Holy Family, while impressing the savages with the greatness of God and of His saints.

Father LeJeune describes one of these feast days at Quebec — that of St. Joseph. "On this day," he writes, "our church was full of devout people, almost as it is on Easter Day, all of them blessing God for having given us as a protector the foster father and guardian angel (so to speak) of Jesus Christ His Son. In my opinion it is through his favor and through his merits that the inhabitants of New France who live upon the banks of the great St. Lawrence River have resolved to receive all the good customs of Old France and to refuse admission to the bad ones."[9] These words of Father LeJeune follow directly upon his description of a fireworks display at Quebec, all in honor of St. Joseph!

Terrible physical hardships beset the missionaries, but all these trials were as nothing compared with the fickleness, the ingratitude, and even the treachery of the savages. The Fathers relied on prayer to get the strength they needed. Since St. Joseph's intercession did not fail them, they could hardly find language to express their gratitude for his friendship.

St. John Brebeuf, later to be martyred for the Faith, tells of some of these difficulties in the founding of the first Huron mission at Ihonatiria. Then he adds, "Several times I was completely baffled and desperate until I had special recourse to our Lord Jesus Christ, for whose glory alone we were undertaking this painful journey, and until I had made a vow to glorious St. Joseph, the new patriarch of the Hurons. Immediately I saw everything become quiet."[10]

LeJeune experienced the same dramatic results while en route to Canada from France. His ship was being driven relentlessly toward the rocks. "If the ship had advanced twenty paces, we would have been dashed to pieces. . . . At the moment when I was offering my vows to God through the medium of this great saint, I was told that the wind had passed by the vessel."[11]

These are but typical instances narrated in the *Jesuit Relations*. Sometimes the missionaries were hopelessly lost in the wilderness until they came to familiar territory after invoking the aid of St. Joseph. Striking favors were granted them in bending the wills of obstinate sinners who had previously expressed only hatred and contempt for the Faith. More than once, droughts were broken after the Fathers asked God to grant their petitions in honor of St. Joseph — and this while the medicine men vainly tried to obtain results from their charms and sorceries.

As an attempt to express their gratitude worthily and also as an additional prayer for the success of their apostolate, the Fathers honored St. Joseph externally as much as possible. Twelve of the converts mentioned in their reports are named after the Saint. The first Huron mission at Ihonatiria was dedicated to him, as well as the first Huron mission at Silery. When Ihonatiria became uninhabitable because of the plague, the new station at Tenaustaye was again called St. Joseph. Lakes, rivers, and other settlements were given the same title.

In this the North American martyrs were merely continuing in the path of the first settlers and missionaries of New France. The Recollect Fathers at Quebec had been responsible for the dedication of the whole land to St. Joseph in 1624. Now, the Jesuits continued to sprinkle "St. Joseph" place names throughout the territory, some of which still remain on the map.

The Pottawatomi and Miami missions at the southeast corner of Lake Michigan influenced the present names of the St. Joseph River, St. Joseph, Michigan, and the adjacent St. Joseph County, Indiana. Lake Michigan itself received the name of Lake St. Joseph from Father Allouez in 1677. Even the part of the Wabash River in lower Illinois and Indiana was described by an early missionary as St. Joseph River. In upper Lake Huron, northwest of Manitoulin Island lies the Isle of St. Joseph, sometimes called Charity Island. There, in 1649 the Jesuits founded a refuge for their Huron Indians in the hope of removing them from the reach of the dreaded Iroquois. As usual, the Fathers dedicated the mission to St. Joseph and the Church to our Lady.

As a final instance of this linking of the names of Joseph and Mary, we can read the words of Jerome Lallemant, S.J. On the Wye River in Canada, he reported, "We have given to this new house the name of St. Mary or Our Lady of the Conception. Since St. Joseph was chosen for the patron of this country, we ought not to have taken any other protectress for our house than his spouse, the Blessed Virgin, lest we separate those whom God had bound together so closely."[12]

Reports like this are paralleled by the records of the Paraguay Reductions, where great blessings and favors were ascribed to St. Joseph's intercession; and also by the reports from the Mariana Islands, where the missionaries placed themselves under the protection of St. Joseph. In Madura, India, the great missionary, Joseph Beschi, S.J., utilized his genius for language in amazing heathen scholars by his poem to St. Joseph, expressed in classically elegant Tamil.

In Mexico, Joseph had been declared special patron of the country as early as 1555 at the First Provincial Synod of Mexico. Thenceforth, his feast was celebrated with great fervor and solemnity — and with the usual display of fireworks — everywhere in Latin America. As is easily noted on the map, particularly on the west coast of North America, the Spanish Franciscans made their missions monuments of devotion to St. Joseph.

On August 17, 1678, Pope Innocent XI confirmed the choice of St. Joseph as special patron of the Chinese missions. On March 19, 1692, the missionaries obtained the written permission of the Emperor to preach the Gospel freely in his territories. In gratitude they determined to erect a votive chapel in honor of St. Joseph although three other churches already existed in Peking.

It was again on the feast of St. Joseph in 1700 that the cornerstone was laid of a chapel in honor of St. Francis Xavier on the island of Sancian; but the votive chapel that had been projected for Peking was not finished until 1721. Its cornerstone bore a dedicatory inscription to St. Joseph written in Latin, Chinese, and Tatar. Then came the dreadful earthquake of 1730, which is said to have taken 500,000 lives. Unlike the three churches in Peking, St. Joseph's votive chapel was almost untouched by the disaster, and none of the Fathers in the three mission houses in the city was harmed.

In the United States one of the first churches in the section under British rule was old St. Joseph's in Philadelphia, founded in 1733 by the Jesuit Josiah Greaton. The conversion of General Ethan Allen's daughter during the late eighteenth century caused a tremendous sensation, especially when she became the first American nun. Frances Allen, when twelve years old, had beheld an unknown man who protected her from harm. Not until thirteen years later did she recognize his identity as that of St. Joseph, to whom she attributed her conversion as well as her vocation. At Emmetsburg, Maryland, Mother Elizabeth Seton placed her community and her loved ones under Joseph's protection, calling her nuns the Sisters of St. Joseph. Her mother house still bears his name. Another pioneer, Bishop Flaget of Bardstown, Kentucky, was wholeheartedly devoted to the Saint and begged him to watch over his struggling diocese and its grave needs.

In our own day Canada received the crowning favor of a basilica that has deservedly been called the most magnificent shrine of St. Joseph in the whole world. It was most fitting that this basilica was erected at Montreal. There, indeed, after the era of the first missionaries the Sulpician Fathers followed in the steps of their founder, Father Olier, by inspiring the faithful to turn to St. Joseph. There, too, the Ursulines and Grey Nuns had always paid the Saint exceptional veneration, for Mother Mary of the Incarnation, foundress of the Ursulines at Quebec, had led the way for her own spiritual daughters and for other holy women in imitating Teresa of Avila not only in sublime contemplation and active zeal but also in love for St. Joseph.

The basilica at Montreal, St. Joseph's Oratory, had its origin in the faith of a lay brother of the Congregation of Holy Cross. Brother André, whose name in the world had been Alfred Bessette, entered the Congregation in 1870 and was assigned the humble post of doorkeeper at Notre Dame College in Montreal. Some day, so he spoke with the certainty of faith, God in His goodness would lift up a monument to St. Joseph on the steep western summit of Mount Royal, across the street from the college.

Hundreds of instances are on record in which people claim to have received miraculous favors after Brother André directed them to pray or to perform some other pious action in honor of St. Joseph. But the truest miracle is the miracle of faith; that a poorly educated and sickly lay brother could have been the human instrument and the moral force responsible for a massive temple of God, second to few buildings of its type and without a doubt the foremost shrine of St. Joseph in the world.

The Oratory itself was founded in 1904. Some ten years later, the crypt structures were begun. The dimensions of the basilica unit are hard to imagine simply for their vastness. On the first level, about fifty feet from the ground, rests the sedate crypt church, three stories high and accommodating two thousand persons. It is, however, dwarfed by the monumental basilica which rises behind it to a height of almost four hundred feet, and capable of holding a congregation of more than ten thousand worshipers. Together with the majestic proportions of the basilica, the policy of con structing the Oratory gradually and according to the funds on hand is reminiscent of the decades required to erect the ageless cathedrals of Europe.

Brother André died in 1937 at the age of 92. He did not live to see the basilica finished, but he saw its future success assured, and with that he was content. St. Joseph's Oratory would rise to the clouds, symbolizing the prayers of the millions of pilgrims who have traveled there to honor and imitate and beg the help of their patron. Brother André liked to call himself "St. Joseph's little dog," but the story of the monument he caused to be created merits for him the title of "Apostle of St. Joseph."

As far as devotional aspects are concerned, the Oratory is already the world-wide shrine of St. Joseph's cultus. But more was needed. There existed a great need for some central organization, an international clearinghouse, as it were, for the "things of St. Joseph." The history of the devotion to St. Joseph is a unique story in the Church. It has had its difficulties not only because of the sparse source material about the Saint, but also because of uncritical writings whose ill-advised attempts to honor St. Joseph were based on exaggerated speculation. Perhaps because of this situation or because of the limited data immediately available, there has existed among Catholics a kind of shying away from deeper study of the problems concerning the Saint. Popular devotion took for granted St. Joseph's position as second to that of Mary, but serious research had not given him full attention.

Accordingly, on April 30, 1952, the feast of the Solemnity of St. Joseph, a charter meeting of some fifty priests, nuns, and laymen was held at the Oratory to discuss organized research on questions concerning the Saint. With the approval of His Eminence, Paul-Emile Cardinal Léger, Archbishop of Montreal, constitutions were drawn up for an official "Research and Documentation Center" whose headquarters would be at the Oratory.

These constitutions stated the purpose of the society: to

encourage a more profound study of the exalted position held by St. Joseph as virginal husband of Mary, as virgin father of Jesus, and as head of the Holy Family. At the library, every available bit of literature extant on St. Joseph was to be collected, either in book form or microfilm. The Center was interested in all Josephite questions, not limiting itself to dogmatic theology alone, but extending its patronage to exegesis, patristics, church history, ascetical and mystical theology, music, sculpture, painting, poetry, and drama — wherever these sciences and arts touch on the person or devotion of St. Joseph.

A similar desire to give the devotion the support of scholarship led to the founding in 1947 of the Spanish periodical, *Estudios Josefinos*. This was issued semiannually by the Discalced Carmelites of Valladolid, and was a sort of counterpart of the semiannual *Cahiers de Joséphologie* published by the Center at Montreal. On August 30, 1951, the Spanish Society of Josephology was officially established. Less than two years later, May 25, 1953, its title was changed to "The Ibero-American Society of Josephology" so that it might include Spain, Portugal, and all New World nations speaking Spanish and Portuguese.

The actual results of these foundations can be known only by time and experience. One conclusion is certain: the devotion to St. Joseph has taken still another step toward full maturity in the Church, removing more and more the obscurity which was required temporarily by St. Joseph's vocation, but now to be replaced by the full appreciation of the man nearest to Jesus Christ.

THE DEVOTION TO ST. JOSEPH IN THE LITURGY

Following the reign of Sixtus IV (1471–1484), the feast of St. Joseph in the Roman church was raised to the rank of a "double," and was so classified by Pope St. Pius V in the reformed breviary.

In 1621, Gregory XV prescribed it as a holyday of obligation, but since his decree was not put into execution everywhere, Urban VIII re-emphasized the public observance of
the feast in 1642. This was all the more remarkable in view
of Urban's desire to limit rather than increase the number
of such holydays.

During these years the saintly Carmelite nun, Clara Maria
of the Passion († 1675), had been urging that the feast of
St. Joseph be given a higher rank in the liturgy, as was more
befitting. Clement X acceded to these requests in 1670, ele-
vating the feast as a "double of the second class."

Although there now existed a special Mass and feast of
St. Joseph, there was still lacking a Divine Office which
would exclusively apply to the Saint. The original Office
of St. Joseph had been introduced during the pontificate of
Innocent VIII (1484–1492); but in 1522 it had been sup-
planted by another, except in the breviaries of the Franciscans. Both of these Offices were abolished by Pius V, who
substituted only the common formulary used for "Confessor"
saints.

When Clement XI became pope in 1700, he felt that he
could not afford to overlook the movement in the Church
toward greater devotion to St. Joseph, a devotion he himself
loved fervently. In his time also, the Franciscan preacher,
Bonaventure da Potenza († 1712), was energetically working
for the greater spread of the devotion and for the more
worthy celebration of the feast. Patrignani's life of St. Joseph could assert that since 1522 more than 300 works on
the Saint had appeared in various languages and localities.
This was all the more remarkable in view of the political
upheavals and the slow printing processes of the times.

Clement XI accordingly responded to this popular desire
by composing a new Office of St. Joseph, prescribed for
Church use in 1714. He was also responsible for the approval
of a votive Mass in honor of St. Joseph, to obtain the grace
of a happy death. This Mass had been composed by the

Theatine, Cardinal Thomasi († 1713). As if in answer to his oft-uttered wish and prayer, Clement died on the feast of St. Joseph, 1721.

Another signal mark of honor was left not for Clement but for his successors to bestow on the Saint. In the Church's Litany of the Saints the name of St. Joseph did not occur. Bologna had placed Joseph's name in its litany of the Saints in 1350, and the Dominicans and Carmelites had done the same in their approved liturgical books ever since the middle of the 1500's. Then in 1684 (as already related), Emperor Leopold I requested Innocent XI to make the insertion. Even when these petitions became more frequent, Clement XI for all his devotion to St. Joseph hesitated to take any action because of a fear of creating the precedent of frequent alteration. Throughout, it was acknowledged that no legitimate reason existed for dropping St. Joseph's name once the custom had appeared of inserting it (see p. 104).

An any rate, Innocent XIII came to the papal throne in 1721, and the question was opened once again. Petitions had now arrived from the Emperor Charles VI, from the Electors of Cologne and the Palatine, from the Grand Count of Etruria, and from forty Superiors or Procurators-General of religious orders. The reasons pro and con had already been studied in great detail in 1714, when Cardinal Prosper Lambertini (the future Benedict XIV) was appointed *promotor fidei,* an official designated to find all possible reasons against the change.

Lambertini's favorable recommendations were again considered. Since Innocent died before he could make the final decision, Benedict XIII acted in 1726, approving the insertion of the name of St. Joseph after that of John the Baptist in the Litany of the Saints.

Beginning with the pontificate of Pius IX, Joseph's rise in the liturgical life of the Church has been meteoric. In 1847, Pius increased the rank of the feast which was known as the Solemnity of St. Joseph, extending it to the whole Church. After numerous other honors for the Saint, the pope took his most notable step in declaring Joseph Patron of the Universal Church in a solemn ceremony that took place on December 8, 1870.

Pope St. Pius X continued the process of exalting St. Joseph in the liturgy. In the years 1911–1913, St. Pius prescribed that the "Solemn Commemoration of St. Joseph, Spouse of the Blessed Virgin Mary and Confessor," was to be observed on March 19. However, since the Lenten penitential season prevented the full celebration of an octave, the pope elevated the rank of the second feast during Paschal time under the title, "The Solemnity of St. Joseph, Spouse of the Blessed Virgin Mary, Confessor, Patron of the Universal Church." (This had been the feast of the Patronage.)

At this juncture certain liturgical writers petitioned that March 19 be reduced to its former rank of "double rite of the second class," since there never had existed any historical reason to celebrate March 19 as the "natal" feast of St. Joseph (that is, the anniversary of his death, his birth into heaven). Moreover, the Saint, so these writers said, was now worthily honored by the feast of the Solemnity.

A decree of October 28, 1913, acceded to this request, and also directed that the feast of the Solemnity should be celebrated on the third Wednesday instead of the third Sunday after Easter. But on December 12, 1917, Pope Benedict XV re-elevated March 19 to its earlier rank of "double rite of the first class," as it stands today.

By a decree of the Congregation of Sacred Rites dated April 24, 1956, the Solemnity of St. Joseph was abolished, and the feast of St. Joseph the Worker was placed in its stead. However, the title of St. Joseph as Patron of the Universal Church was to be added to his "principal feast," March 19.[13]

The feast of Joseph the Worker was first announced by Pius XII in an address given on the occasion of the tenth anniversary of the Christian Association of Italian Workers, May 1, 1955. "From the beginning," he stated, "We put your organization under the powerful patronage of St. Joseph. Indeed there could be no better protector to help deepen in your lives the spirit of the Gospel. As we said then [March 11, 1945], that spirit flows to you and all men from the heart of the God-man, Savior of the world; but certainly, no worker was ever more completely and profoundly penetrated by it than the foster father of Jesus, who lived with Him in closest intimacy and community of family life and work. Thus, if you wish to be close to Christ, We again today repeat, 'Go to Joseph' (Genesis 41:44).

"Yes, beloved workers, the Pope and the Church cannot withdraw from the divine mission of guiding, protecting, and loving especially the suffering, who are all the more dear the more they are in need of defence and help, whether they be workers or other children of the people.

"This duty and obligation We, the Vicar of Christ, desire to declare again clearly here on this first day of May, which the world of labor has claimed for itself as its own proper feast day. We intend that all may recognize the dignity of labor, and that this dignity may be the motive in forming the social order and the law founded on the equitable distribution of rights and duties.

"Acclaimed in this way by Christian workers, and having received, as it were, Christian baptism, the first of May — far from being an incitation to discord, hate, and violence — is and will be a recurring invitation to modern society to accomplish what is still lacking for social peace; a Christian feast, therefore, that is, a day of rejoicing for the concrete and progressive triumph of the Christian ideals of the great family of all who labor.

"In order that this meaning may remain in your minds and that in some way We may make an immediate return for the many and precious gifts brought to Us from all parts of Italy, We are happy to announce to you Our determination to institute — as We in fact do now institute — the liturgical feast of St. Joseph the Worker, assigning it to the first day of May. Are you pleased with this Our gift, beloved workers? We are certain that you are, because the humble workman of Nazareth not only personifies before God and the Church the dignity of the man who works with his hands, but he is always the provident guardian of you and your families."[14]

The archbishops and bishops of the United States at their annual meeting in 1955 petitioned the Holy See for permission to use the mass of this feast of St. Joseph on Labor Day in September, inasmuch as Labor Day represented the popular celebration of what May Day represented in other countries. By an indult of the Congregation of Sacred Rites dated February 25, 1956, this permission was granted for the next ten years. Therefore, unless impeded by feasts of high rank, the mass of St. Joseph the Worker may be celebrated in the United States and its territories according to the conditions of this indult on the first Monday in September. It should be noted, however, that this arrangement does not affect the obligatory use of the proper Mass and Office assigned to May 1 with the rank of double of the first class.

Occasionally the Holy See has been forced to condemn or to prohibit exaggerations that do not represent true devotion to St. Joseph because they infringe on the exclusive positions of Mary and of Jesus. None the less, a cursory glance at the list of honors heaped on the Saint by recent popes reveals that the Church seems to be placing more and more emphasis on St. Joseph's position as set apart from other saints.

Perhaps the greatest of these exclusive honors consists in the Litany of St. Joseph, which was promulgated on March 18, 1909, when Pius X sanctioned its use in public services. Only four other litanies in the Church have been granted such approval (as we mentioned on p. 91): the Litanies of the Sacred Heart and of the Holy Name of Jesus, the Blessed Virgin's Litany of Loreto, and the Litany of the Saints.

In 1919 Benedict XV approved the Preface of St. Joseph, to be used in all Masses in honor of the Saint. In the Latin Rite, we note, no other saint except Mary is given such a special Preface. St. Joseph was again singled out in 1921 when Benedict ordered the phrase inserted into the Divine Praises, "Blessed be St. Joseph, her most chaste spouse." The following year, Pius XI inserted the name of St. Joseph in the Church's official prayers for the dying.

The future is in the hands of God; but undoubtedly the Holy Spirit will not cease honoring him to whom the Church applies the words, "A faithful man shall be greatly praised, and he that is the keeper of his Lord shall be glorified."[15] John Gerson and other pioneers of the devotion never dared in their wildest dreams to fancy anything half so bold as the present reality, and what the future still suggests.

REFERENCES — APPENDIX

(The topics of this section are suggested by and partly based on Otto Pfülf, "Die Verehrung des hl. Joseph in der Geschichte," in *Stimmen aus Maria-Laach*, 38 [1890], 283–302.)

1. Ignatius of Loyola, Letter 135.

2. *The Life of St. Teresa of Jesus, Written by Herself*, tr. Lewis, ed. Zimmerman, Newman, Westminster (Maryland), 1943; 32, 14; 33, 14; 33, 16; cf. *Acta Sanctorum Octobris*, 7 *passim*.

3. Francis de Sales, *The Spiritual Conferences*, tr. by Sisters of the Visitation (London: Burns, Oates and Washbourne, 1909), 368.

4. The foregoing statistics are calculated from art. "Joseph," in *Lexikon für Theologie und Kirche*, ed. Hofmann, Buchberger, Herder, Freiburg im Breisgau, 1935, 5, 565–570.

5. Tr. from Pfülf, 294, who quotes O. Klopp, *Das Jahr 1683*, Graz.

6. The pertinent documents of the controversy are printed in Benedict XIV, 4, 2, c. 14, No. 11. For Leo XIII's letter to Spain, *ASS* 22, 462; to Portugal, *Sanc. Dom. N. Leonis Papae XIII, Allocutiones, Epistolae, Constitutiones*, Desclée de Brouwer, 1894, 4, 53 (June 3, 1890).

7. Vincent Baesten in *Précis historique*, Brussels, tom. 28 (1879), 196, 203.

8. Tr. from *Oeuvres Oratoires de Bossuet*, ed. Lebarq, Desclée, Paris, 1927, 2, 127, 133, 140; pts. 1, 2, 3 of the "First Panegyric."

9. This account follows *The Jesuit Relations and Allied Documents*, ed. R. G. Thwaites, Burrows, Cleveland, 1896–1901; here, Relation of 1637; 2, 67. For other favors and marks of devotion to St. Joseph on the missions, cf.

Antonio Savani, S.J., *S. Giuseppe e la Compagnia di Gesu*, Bassano, 1950, 206–252.

  10. Relation of 1635; 8, 73.
  11. Relation of September 10, 1640; 18, 69.
  12. Relation of May 27, 1640; 19, 137.
  13. *AAS*, 48, 237.
  14. Cf. ref. 27, Ch. 1.
  15. Chapter at Vespers, March 19; cf. Prov. 28:20, 27:18.

Resolutions of the Session of Studies Held at St. Joseph's Oratory, Montreal, August 1–9, 1955.

TO FITTINGLY conclude this session of studies which has grouped together some 38 representatives from all the principal countries of the West, the members of this group respectfully suggest:

1) That meetings of theologians and historians interested in questions of Josephology be organized in all countries, as already has been realized in Spain, Mexico, and Canada.

2) That a series of courses or a study club on questions pertaining to St. Joseph be introduced in all major seminaries and scholasticates, or at least that special mention be made of these problems in the treatise on Mariology.

3) That theological, biblical, and Marian societies take greater interest in these questions concerning St. Joseph.

4) That the feast of the Espousals of Mary and Joseph (January 23) be extended to the Universal Church.

5) That the privilege, already accorded to the Oblates of Mary Immaculate, of commemorating St. Joseph on all feast days and in all offices of the Blessed Virgin might be granted to all who ask for it.

6) That, in conformity with the desire of hundreds of bishops and thousands of the faithful, the name of St. Joseph be introduced into the prayers of the Mass (*Confiteor, Suscipe Sancta Trinitas, Communicantes,* and *Libera*

Nos), or at least into the *Confiteor,* and in the corresponding prayers of the Eastern Rites.

7) That, according to the desire of the Ukrainian Catholics of the Byzantine Rite present at this meeting, a special feast of St. Joseph be instituted in their liturgy.

8) That, in addition to the traditional titles of "putative father" and "foster father," we should not be reluctant to make use of the expression "virgin father," employed in the prayer approved by St. Pius X.

Bibliography

BOOKS

Benedict XIV, *De Beatificatione Servorum Dei et Canonizatione Beatorum,* Venice, 1767, 4, 2.

Bover, Joseph M., S.J., *De Cultu S. Iosephi Amplificando* (Barcelona: Subirana, 1926).

Bucceroni, Ianuarius, S.J., *Commentarii de SS. Corde Iesu, de Beata Virgine Maria, et de S. Iosepho,* ed. 4 (Rome: Polyglot, 1896).

Cantera, Eugenio, O.A.R., *San José en el plan divino* (Monachil: Santa Rita, 1917).

Démaret, Gaston, O.S.B., *Marie de qui est né Jésus,* tom. 6, "Saint Joseph," (Paris: Spes, 1939).

Dubois, Cardinal, *Saint Joseph,* ed. 9 (Paris: Gabalda, 1928).

Filas, Francis L., S.J., *Joseph and Jesus* (Milwaukee: Bruce, 1952).

——— *The Family for Families* (Milwaukee: Bruce, 1947).

——— *The Man Nearest to Christ* (Milwaukee: Bruce, 1944).

Herrmann, R. P., C.Ss.R., *Institutiones Theologiae Dogmaticae,* ed. 7 (Lyons: Vitte, 1937), 6.

Herve, Can. J. M., *Manuale Theologiae Dogmaticae,* ed. 17, 4 tom. (Paris: Berche et Pagis, 1935) (tom. 2, 649–653; St. Joseph).

Holzmeister, Urban, S.J., *De Sancto Ioseph Quaestiones Biblicae* (Rome: Pont. Inst. Bibl., 1945).

Jugie, Martin, A. A., *La Mort et l'assomption de la sainte vierge,* Vatican City, 1944.

Lépicier, Alexius H. Card., O.S.M., *Tractatus de Sancto Ioseph,* ed. 1 (Paris: Lethielleux, 1908), ed. 3 (Rome: Buona Stampa, 1933).

Lercher, L., S.J., *Institutiones Theologiae Dogmaticae,* ed. 4 (Barcelona: Herder, 1945), 3.

Llamera, Bonifacio, O.P., *Teología de San José,* La Editorial Catolica (Madrid: Biblioteca de autores cristianos, 1954).

Macabiau, Cyprien, S.J. ("C. Mariani," "C.M."), *De Cultu Sancti Josephi Amplificando — Postulatum* (Paris: Gabalda, 1908).

——— *Primauté de Saint Joseph d'aprés l'épiscopat catholique et la théologie,* reprint (Montreal: Fides, 1945).

Marchesi, Aloysius, *Amplificationis Cultus Sancti Josephi Beatae Mariae Virginis Sponsi* (Rome: Marietti, 1870).

Mercier, P. V., S.J., *Saint Joseph* (Paris: Lethielleux, 1895).

Mitterer, Albert, *Dogma und biologie der heiligen familie* (Vienna: Herder, 1953).

Morales, Petrus, S.J., *In Caput Primum Matthaei,* lib. 5 (Paris: Vivès, 1869).

Mueller, Joseph, S.J., *Der heilige Joseph — die dogmatischen Grundlagen seiner besonderen Verehrung* (Innsbruck: Rauch, 1937). In English: *The Fatherhood of St. Joseph,* tr. by Athanasius Dengler, O.S.B. (St. Louis: Herder, 1952).

Papebroch, Daniel, S.J., *Acta Sanctorum Martii,* Antwerpiae, 1668, 3.

Rondet, Henri, S.J., *Saint Joseph, Textes anciens avec une introduction* (Paris: Lethielleux, 1954).

Sauvé, Charles, S.S., *Saint Joseph Intime*, ed. 4 (Paris: de Gigord, 1920).

Savani, Antonio, S.J., *S. Giuseppe e la Compagnia di Gesu*, Bassano, 1950.

Seitz, Joseph, *Die Verehrung des heiligen Joseph in ihrer geschichtlichen Entwicklung bis zum Konzil von Trient* (Freiburg im Breisgau: Herder, 1908).

Sinibaldi, Msgr. Giacomo, *La Grandezza di San Giuseppe* (Rome: Tip. Pol. Cuore di Maria, 1927).

Vivès, Fr. Iosephus Calasanctius Card., O.M.Cap., *Summa Iosephina* (Rome: Pont. Inst. Pii IX, 1907).

ARTICLES

Anon., *L'Ami du Clergé*, 34 (1912), 217–220, response on dignity of St. Joseph.

Anon., *L'Ami du Clergé*, 53 (1936), 549–551, response on the assumption of St. Joseph.

Alastruey, D. Gregorio, "Teología de San José," in *Estudios Josefinos*, 1 (1947), 9–34.

Dusserre, Joseph, "Les origines de la devotion à saint Joseph," in *Cahiers de Joséphologie*, 1 (1953), 23–54; 169–196; 2 (1954), 5–30.

Ermoni, V., "Joseph, Saint," in Vigoroux, *Dictionaire de la Bible*, Paris, 1903, 3, 1670.

Galdos, R., S.J., "S. Joseph sanctitas et dignitas ex locis evangelicis probata," in *Verbum Domini*, 7 (1927), 133–137.

Garrigou-Lagrange, Reginald, O.P., "De Praestantia Sancti Joseph inter omnes Sanctos," in *Angelicum*, 5 (1928), 195–212. In French: "La Prééminence de saint Joseph sur tout autre saint," in *La Vie Spirituelle*, 19 (1928), 662–683.

José Antonio del Nino Jesús, O.C.D., "También Asunción de San José?" in *Estudios Josefinos*, 4 (1950), 147–149.

Llamera, Bonifacio, O.P., "La dignidad y excelencia de San José," in *Estudios Josefinos*, 4 (1950), 44–68.

——— "Introducción a la teología de San José," in *Ciencia Tomista*, 66 (1944), 255–275.

——— "La paternidad de San José en la teología católica," in *Estudios Josefinos*, 5 (1951), 205–235.

——— "Plenitud de la gracia de San José," in *Estudios Josefinos*, 2 (1948), 164–186.

——— "La santidad essencial de San José," in *Estudios Josefinos*, 5 (1951), 19–38.

Michel, A., "Joseph, Saint," in Vacant-Mangenot-Amann, *Dictionnaire de théologie catholique*, Letouzey, Paris, 1925, 8, 1510–1521.

O'Carroll, Michael, "St. Joseph in the Church," in *Irish Ecclesiastical Record*, 85 (1956), 252–260.

Reimsbach, Joseph A., S.J., "Le patronage de S. Joseph," in *Gregorianum*, 2 (1921), 337–351.

Rondet, Henri, S.J., "Saint Joseph, histoire et théologie," in *Nouvelle Revue Théologique*, 75 (1953), 113–140. This article appears in English in Rondet, Henri, S.J., *Saint Joseph*, ed. by Donald Attwater (New York: Kenedy), 1956, 3–54.

Index